YOU CAN

Teach
your class to
LISTEN

Sue Palmer

FOR AGES
7-11

"Listening must be planned for, taught, developed and assessed"
DfES

Acknowledgements

Author
Sue Palmer

Editor
Kathleen McCully

Project Editor
Fabia Lewis

Series Designer
Joy Monkhouse

Design and Illustrations
Q2A Media

Cover illustration
© BrandX/Punchstock

Text © Sue Palmer
© 2007 Scholastic Ltd

Designed using Adobe InDesign

Published by Scholastic Ltd
Villiers House
Clarendon Avenue
Leamington Spa
Warwickshire CV32 5PR

www.scholastic.co.uk

Printed by Bell and Bain Ltd.
1 2 3 4 5 6 7 8 9   7 8 9 0 1 2 3 4 5 6

You Can Teach Your Class to Listen is based on the author's research for a previous book – *Toxic Childhood: How the Modern World is Damaging our Children … and What We Can Do About it* (Sue Palmer © 2006 Orion) – in which she brought together the work of a range of academics concerned with child development and language and listening skills acquisition. This included neuroscientists, Early Years specialists, developmental psychologists, linguistics experts and speech and language therapists.

The teaching ideas in *You Can Teach Your Class to Listen,* are the result of five years of meetings with Early Years teachers, around the UK. This book is therefore dedicated to all those teachers, who shared their practice so generously. S.P

British Library Cataloguing-in-Publication Data
A catalogue record for this book is available from the British Library.

ISBN 978-0439-94533-2

The right of Sue Palmer to be identified as the author of this work has been asserted by her in accordance with the Copyright, Designs and Patents Act 1988.

Extracts from The National Literacy Strategy © Crown copyright. Reproduced under the terms of HMSO Guidance Note 8.

Thanks to Sarah Bott, deputy headteacher at St Martin's Church of England Primary, Tipton, West Midlands, for permission to use her 'goggles' idea on page 39.

Contents

Contents

Introduction

This book owes its existence to a teacher in Yorkshire whom I met about seven years ago. During an inservice session I was running on writing across the curriculum, she said: 'We've got this all the wrong way round. They can't write till they can talk. And they can't talk till they can listen. And they can't bloody listen!'

This truth, once uttered, was so self-evident it changed the entire direction of my life as a literacy specialist. I became obsessed with speaking and listening, but especially the Cinderella of the duo – listening skills. I found myself seeking out speech and language therapists, who have specific expertise in the acquisition of speaking and listening skills, and educational psychologists with insights into attention deficit disorder. But they pointed me further, towards neuroscience and brain development, and experts in these fields showed me that the roots of effective listening go very deep. Balance, physical coordination and control are part of the picture, as are aspects of short- and long-term memory.

How can I teach my class to listen?

First of all, you have to be clear what listening involves. People who grew up in the days when listening developed naturally are not usually aware of how good they are at listening, and why. So your own understanding of the elements involved is probably implicit rather than explicit. **Chapter 1** defines the skills that make a good listener so that you can target them for all your class, and spot those children who need more help in particular areas. **Chapter 2** helps you to listen more effectively yourself, and to model good listening skills. **Chapters 3 to 5** suggest a range of opportunities for developing specific skills through a variety of teaching and learning activities. Most activities involve the use of listening skills to help fulfil other curricular objectives. **Chapter 6** continues the theme of listening throughout the school day, looking at generic organisational and teaching methods and suggestions for assessment.

These suggestions are only starting points. Once you are aware of what good listening involves, you can look for other ways of targeting the key skills to ensure their steady, incremental development in all your pupils.

You Can... **Help children sit still**

In order to sit still and listen, children need physical coordination and control, and opportunities to run off excess energy.

Thinking points

● Children's attention skills depend upon their body awareness, balance and physical coordination, which all develop through opportunities to move about freely. They need to learn control of big movements, which leads to an increase in fine motor coordination, control and balance. Since many children today lead a sedentary existence, we have to provide opportunities for movement at school.

● The ability to be still depends on a mature vestibular system (our inner sense of body awareness and balance). When you ask children to sit in a space and some insist on leaning against furniture or each other, it could be because a poorly-developed sense of their body's position in space means they need to make contact with a surface to help them balance.

● For more information on how movement underpins behaviour, language and learning, see:
  ○ www.jabadao.org
  ○ *The Well-Balanced Child* by Sally Goddard Blythe (Hawthorn Press).

Tips, ideas and activities

● Make sure you provide lots of opportunities for movement in the school day, through PE, drama and dance. This may seem a long way from sitting still and listening, but physical self-awareness and control is the bedrock of attention.

● As well as your regular PE session, encourage outdoor education and active play. Playtime should provide opportunities for children to run off excess energy and take part in spontaneous PE. There should be appropriate space to run and jump and for play equipment that allows children to climb, balance, skip and so on. Make sure senior management are aware of the importance of active outdoor play in developing listening and attention skills, to encourage them to invest in the school's outdoor environment. Learning through Landscapes (www.ltl.org.uk) is a helpful source of advice.

● Whatever you are studying, look for ways of integrating activities involving controlled movement, for example:
  ○ slow-motion miming of a process, such as the development of a caterpillar into a butterfly (if you can find suitable music to accompany this type of activity, it will be even more effective)
  ○ miming or creating a series of 'living tableaux' scenes from history or the book you are sharing.

● Use Brain Gym activities in breaks between lessons. Cross-lateral movements (alternately moving opposite sides of the body) are believed to forge strong links between the two hemispheres of the brain.

● In music lessons, encourage children to move to music. Let them:
  ○ move freely to the music, choosing their own movements
  ○ copy simple sequences of movements that you show them.
There are many other ways of encouraging movement to music on page 27.

● Keep an eye on children with attention problems during all these activities. What sort of coordination tasks do they have trouble with? How can you devise activities that will help them improve their physical control?

You Can... **Help children discriminate sounds**

In an increasingly noisy world, we can no longer assume the natural development of children's ability to make fine discriminations between sounds (essential for literacy).

Thinking points

● Traffic noise outdoors and noise from TV and other electronic equipment indoors is seriously undermining many children's ability to discriminate sounds.

● Both spoken language and literacy skills depend on children being able to discriminate the 44 phonemes of English. They can only learn to do this if they have plenty of 'data' to work on. That data comes from being in an environment rich in language, songs and rhymes, and one which offers plenty of individual attention from adults, particularly in the early years. The best way to provide this is to convince parents of the importance of spending time talking, listening and reading to their children.

Tips, ideas and activities

● The most basic type of sound discrimination is the ability to single out a foreground sound against background noise. If children cannot do that, they will not be able to listen to your voice against background sounds of the classroom. Games like 'Dodgems' help train their ears to listen for specific sounds, while also providing an opportunity to move and let off steam:

  ● You need a whistle, or anything that makes a distinctive noise.
  ● Tell the children they are going to be dodgem cars rushing around making a noise, but not bumping into each other. When they hear the whistle, they must stop immediately.

● Take the class on a 'Listening Walk' around the school and the school environment. Stop every so often and listen for, say, 15 seconds. How many sounds can the children hear and identify?

● As a 'filler' activity between lessons, try playing 'Sharp Ears'. Ask the children to be absolutely silent for a minute, and see how many different sounds they can hear. At the end of the minute, let them pool the sounds they detected.

● Try to integrate the use of sounds and sound effects into your teaching across the curriculum. There are many suggestions for doing this through music (page 29) and literacy (page 37), but you can find opportunities to focus on sounds, and the differences between sounds, throughout the curriculum. For instance, when conducting science experiments, encourage children to listen (and report on what they hear) as well as look.

You Can... Teach social listening skills

Social listening includes making eye contact, taking turns, and listening actively and responsively to whoever is speaking to you. It usually happens in pairs or small groups of speakers, but class activities involve social listening in a large group too.

Thinking points

• In some cultures, eye contact is considered impolite, so you will have to explain (to children and parents) that in school it is both acceptable and necessary. Poor eye contact can be a result of too much screen-based activity outside school. Disturbingly, British research found that a majority of six- to eight-year-olds preferred to look at a blank screen rather than a human face.

• Good social listening skills are part and parcel of good manners – they demonstrate that the listener has respect for the speaker and his or her point of view. Good listening therefore underpins not only children's educational success, but also social and behavioural success. It is therefore worth investing a great deal of time and energy in developing these skills.

Tips, ideas and activities

• Discuss social skills with your class and compile a list of what makes a good listener in everyday life. Talk about why certain conventions, such as making eye contact and turn-taking, are important.

• Use circle time to practise these skills (see page 23). For instance:
  - If there are children in your class who find it difficult to make eye contact, provide activities (such as 'passing a look around the circle') to help them get used to it
  - To establish turn-taking conventions, have a special object (like the conch in *Lord of the Flies*) which is passed around to signify whose turn it is to speak.

• If children have difficulty looking directly at you during class time, try using eye contact as a way of granting small privileges, for example: *When everyone's ready, it's home-time. Sit up straight and when I'm ready to let you go and get your coat, I'll look at you.* It is amazing how desperate they can be to look you straight in the eye on such occasions. But remember that eye contact during class lessons is not necessarily an indication that a child is listening – research has shown that many children (especially boys) find it easier to concentrate when they are not looking at the teacher. These sorts of issues need discussing.

• Also discuss what is involved in *actively* listening during a conversation. This is not easy to define, and all too often is reduced to simple descriptions of outward behaviour, for example: *Sit still, look at the speaker, ask questions if you don't understand.* But it actually involves the concerted use of all the listening skills described in this chapter to:
  - focus on the speaker and his or her message
  - make sense of what he or she is saying (asking questions if necessary)
  - internalise the information and remember it.

One critical factor in rallying these skills is motivation – you have to *want* to listen. This, of course, has implications for the speaker! (And in terms of class teaching, this very often means YOU.)

You Can... Develop children's auditory memory

We learn and remember through visual, kinaesthetic and auditory channels, but children growing up in a multimedia age often need help to develop their powers of auditory memory.

Thinking points

● One of the most important learning mechanisms is *repetition*. The more children repeat something, the stronger the neural network established in the brain.

● But *meaning* is also important. As well as being able to parrot words and numbers, children need to understand the underlying concepts. If there is no real concept to be understood, it helps to make one up (for example, creating a silly sentence like *Does Olive Eat Sausages?* to remember the spelling of 'does').

● While auditory memory may be poor in children growing up in a multimedia age, visual memory is often strong. Given plenty of opportunities for movement and outdoor play, children also develop kinaesthetic and spatial memory. The more we can link auditory memory to these other ways of remembering, the more powerful their memory and learning as a whole will become.

Tips, Ideas and activities

● School-based learning (especially literacy and numeracy) is highly dependent on auditory memory, remembering:
  ● individual words, such as names and technical vocabulary
  ● sequences of words, such as the months of the year
  ● sequences of numbers, such as number bonds and times tables
  ● sequences of sounds, such as phonemes (*b-l-a-ck*) or syllables (*re-pre-sen-ta-tion*)
  ● patterns of sound and cadences, such as the rhythms of well-formed sentences and particular sentence constructions (for example: *On the one hand…; on the other…*).

● To help children commit useful information to memory, use tricks like:
  ● rhythmic chanting by the whole class (lots of times)
  ● singing it (there are plenty of alphabet and tables songs, but you can also make up your own songs, by putting your own words to a simple familiar tune)
  ● adding actions, for instance, when learning spelling rules such as those for adding *ing* to a verb, give each an action:
  doubling letters – hold up both arms while saying *double*
  dropping final e – make a chopping action while saying *drop the e*
  changing y to i – with wrists together and fingertips apart, make a Y shape with hands, then bring hands together, as if in prayer, while saying *y to i*.

● Develop children's powers of auditory memory through constant practice by:
  ● asking them to learn rhymes or poems every week (see page 36)
  ● expecting them to build up a repertoire of songs (see page 30).

You Can... **Develop children's imaging skills**

Many thinking and learning skills depend upon powers of mental imagery, which is often closely associated with listening skills.

Thinking points

● In the past, when adults entertained children with stories, rhymes and songs, mental imagery developed naturally in most children who 'made their own pictures' while they listened. But the availability of vivid images on TV, DVDs and websites, as well as beautifully produced picture books, means today's children do not have the same opportunities to develop this skill. In fact, some children do not even know it is possible to make their own mental pictures.

● However, the accessibility of images, icons and symbols today provides children with a ready-made visual library on which to draw when making their own mental pictures. Your task as a teacher is to help them understand what mental imaging is, and build up their skills in using the contents of their 'picture library'.

Tips, ideas and activities

● Find out how good your class is at 'making pictures in their heads' by asking them to stare at a blank space on the wall. Then read them a short description or poem such as 'Windy Nights' (see photocopiable page 56) and ask them to *Make your own picture*. Give them a couple of minutes to describe their picture to a 'talking partner' and compare the images they produced. Ask a few pairs to feed back to the class.

● The first time you do this, some children may find it difficult. Often there are several who seem to expect an image to appear on the wall, as if someone had switched on a TV. But as these non-visualisers hear children who *are* able to imagine talk about the 'pictures in their heads', they generally get the idea.

● Always be on the lookout for ways to develop this skill through other listening activities across the curriculum:
  ○ In maths, ask children to imagine five rabbits, six rabbits, and so on (and clap/blink/tap on the table for each rabbit they can see in their heads).
  ○ In PSHE, help children visualise a calm, quiet, special place that they can go to in their heads when things get too much for them (page 24).
  ○ When revising an activity, ask children to close their eyes and visualise what they did yesterday.

● Use 'skeleton planning frameworks' (see photocopiable page 58) for organising and recording information across the curriculum. Internalising these six visual structures helps children visualise information spatially to aid recall, for example, along a time line for a sequence of events, or on the legs of a spidergram for separate categories of information. When recounting or reporting the information orally or in writing, they can use:
  ○ visual imagery to help them organise the information
  ○ auditory memory of the words and phrases needed to convey it.

You Can... Build up children's listening stamina

Teaching children to listen involves building listening stamina so that they can attend for increasingly long periods. This requires an incremental approach.

Thinking points

● Children accustomed to a multimedia world are not used to attending for long. If they miss something on DVD or CD, they can just rewind and replay. If something is boring, they can fast-forward or change channels. We have to teach them how to attend when it matters.

● Several teachers have told me that, when they first introduced oral maths or dictation (see page 38), the children found it so taxing that they began to cry. The way to avoid such stress is thoughtful incremental teaching, with plenty of praise for achievement at each stage.

● Poor listening skills are often at the root of behavioural problems. The more you are aware of the problems children are encountering, the better you can break down your teaching to accommodate them.

Tips, ideas and activities

● Children need gradual training to build up listening stamina, especially those with poor attention spans. Gauge what is a reasonable length of time to expect the class as a whole to concentrate on oral work, and give plenty of praise when they reach or exceed your expectations.

● You can specifically aim to build up listening stamina during:
  ○ circle time, by steadily increasing the length of activities or of the sentence frames you expect them to use as they 'pass a sentence around the circle' (see page 22)
  ○ class novel time, gradually reading for longer periods (see page 33)
  ○ activities like dictation or oral maths lessons, which should start off very brief (a single sentence of dictation or just two maths questions) and gradually grow longer as the class becomes more competent.

● But be aware of the importance of listening stamina across the curriculum. Whenever you introduce a new activity involving listening, start with short bursts. Make the activity as easy as possible by being sure about:
  ○ exactly what you want to convey
  ○ what you require of the children
  ○ that it is something they are likely to succeed at.
Then be very clear (and brief) in introducing and explaining it. On the next occasion, revise briefly, and then take the learning further. As children develop their skills and understanding, extend the length of time you continue your teaching. This applies both to small groups and the whole class.

● Another way to reduce the challenge is to decrease the size of the group. For instance, watch out for children who have trouble with listening games or activities in the whole class, and arrange for them to practise (and succeed) in a smaller group first, perhaps supervised by a teaching assistant. The confidence of succeeding in the small group situation should set them up for success when they rejoin the class.

You Can... **Help children internalise new vocabulary**

Learning in any area relies on remembering the relevant vocabulary – and this, of course, involves children listening to and internalising the words. You can make it easier for them to succeed by carefully structuring your teaching.

Thinking points

• Children's *receptive vocabulary* consists of the words they recognise in context, and is usually much larger than their *expressive* vocabulary, which consists of the words they actually use. For words to move into their expressive vocabulary, children need thorough understanding of them, and opportunities to use them in context. When children just hear new words, it usually goes 'in one ear and out the other'.

• Researchers at London University have found that explicit teaching of vocabulary in the way described above leads not only to improvements in expressive vocabulary, but also – interestingly – to more sophisticated use of language in general.

Tips, ideas and activities

• When introducing a new theme or topic, make a list of the key vocabulary you want children to remember. Science work on Light and Shadow, for instance, would include words like *transparent*, *opaque* and *translucent*. Target one or two words at a time (with opposites like *transparent* and *opaque*, two words can be easier than one, but make sure *transparent* is well-embedded before introducing an easily confusable word like *translucent*).

   • Always introduce vocabulary within a meaningful context, if possible with visual support such as objects, pictures or demonstrations.

   • When you introduce the word, explicitly state its meaning, and ask the class to repeat it in chorus. (*So if you can see right through it, it's transparent. Transparent. Let's repeat that together… transparent, transparent…very good. Can you say it for me, James? What does it mean, Sana?*)

   • Give plenty of opportunities for children to repeat the word, and talk about it. (*With your talking partner, think of three materials that are transparent and three that are opaque… If there were no opaque materials in the world, how would it affect us?*)

   • Set up activities in which children are able to use the word and concept within a meaningful context (for instance, collecting objects, shining a torch on them and categorising as *transparent*, *translucent* or *opaque*).

• Ensure the class and all interested adults are aware of key vocabulary by adding it to a 'words of the week' poster. Let parents know about it by sending home a note of new vocabulary learned each week and encouraging them to ask their child to explain it.

You Can... **Teach literate language structures**

Children naturally learn the structures of language through listening, imitating and then innovating on familiar patterns. We can use this sequence to introduce them to the patterns of written language that they need for writing and for literate use of spoken language.

Thinking points

● Speech is interactive and produced within a shared context, so it is fragmented and disorganised.

● Writing is produced for an unknown, unseen audience, so it has to be explicit, complex and crafted. It requires a wider vocabulary than speech and we organise it into sentences which become increasingly complex as we express increasingly complex ideas.

● Teaching literacy is about moving children from spoken to written language patterns. By adapting the natural *listen – imitate – innovate* strategy through which they learned to talk in the first place, we can help them to 'talk like a book', using literate language and standard English.

● Since written language is so much more complex than spoken language, children need plenty of help to internalise the patterns *before* being expected to write them.

Tips, ideas and activities

● Written language patterns are very different from the spoken language patterns children use on a day-to-day basis – indeed, most speech is not even in the form of sentences. But if children are to write fluently, they need to be sensitised to the sentence structures of written language. Ensure all children are exposed to literate patterns by using the *listen – imitate – innovate* technique as part of your teaching.

● Two key times to target the use of literate language are:
  ● circle time, where you can introduce 'sentence frames'(see page 25)
  ● literacy, where reading to children and giving opportunities for them to read aloud provides opportunities for *listening* and *imitating* (see pages 41–42).
But, as usual, you can use the technique across the curriculum, ensuring the written sentence structures they need are firmly embedded in children's heads, to provide a basis on which they can *innovate* to express ideas for themselves.

● Indeed, children's real understanding of the term 'sentence' does not come from explanations about full stops and 'making complete sense' but from:
  ● *listening* to lots of sentences, so that they have the echoes and rhythms in their heads
  ● *imitating* sentences, so they hear the patterns issuing from their own mouths (the power of repetition helps here as usual)
  ● *innovating* on these patterns to express their own ideas.
  ● For more information and collections of literate language structures, see *Speaking Frames* by Sue Palmer (David Fulton) for Year 3, 4, 5 and 6 (Scottish Primary, 4, 5, 6 and 7).

You Can... **Invite children to devise listening rules**

Teaching children to listen means modelling genuine listening yourself. This involves treating all members of the class with respect, and actively listening to their ideas.

Thinking points

● If children are involved in devising rules of behaviour, their 'ownership' of these rules means they are more likely to follow them. It also creates strong normative pressures on children who are likely to break them. The technique described here is called 'dialogic teaching', and involves giving children opportunities to engage in dialogue (see page 15 for a further description).

● However, involving children in decision- and rule-making in this way does not mean abnegating responsibility for their behaviour or learning. You are still in charge. The key is to balance:

  ● *warmth* (listening and responding to children and their views, motivating them and raising their self-esteem) and

  ● *firmness* (ensuring there are clear boundaries for behaviour and that children keep to them, and that you cover all your teaching objectives).

Tips, ideas and activities

● As soon as you feel confident enough about teaching listening, declare your room a 'Listening Classroom'. Invite children to think about what good listening involves, and give them two minutes to discuss it with a partner. Then ask some to feed back the results of their deliberations to the class, and use this feedback to begin compiling a list of 'listening rules', inviting other children to add further suggestions. Actively listen to all their deliberations (see page 16).

● Do not be tempted to influence the rules yourself or – even worse – just to make up and impose listening rules. It is more important that the children think hard about what listening involves, and come up with their own suggestions. If these are unworkable, explain why and let them work out alternative ideas.

● Once you have determined the rules, explain that from now on everyone will be expected to abide by the listening rules, including you (this is a good motivation for you to ensure that you do not write down anything *you* cannot abide by). Explain also that everyone should keep an eye (and ear) on how the rules are working, and the class will be able to adapt or add to the rules as you learn more.

● Provide regular opportunities to revisit your listening rules, and make frequent assessments of how they are going (see page 55).

You Can... **Use dialogic teaching techniques**

Teaching through dialogue builds on the popular 'talking partners' strategy. It means every child has a chance to be both speaker and listener, to formulate ideas and come to an understanding through interactivity with peers and teacher.

Thinking points

● Children need opportunities to try out language to express their ideas. Adults can develop vocabulary by introducing words relevant to the situation and explaining them carefully. But children will not internalise vocabulary unless they can use it themselves in a meaningful context.

● The role of the teacher during dialogic teaching is that of a sensitive managing director chairing a discussion. However, remember that teachers have many other roles, depending on the circumstances and learning objective. For example:

  ○ sometimes you just have to tell the children something, because they do not know it yet (see example on page 12)

  ○ sometimes you are like a ringmaster organising activities, or a referee ensuring that everything is done by the rules.

● See also *Towards Dialogic Teaching* by Robin Alexander (Dialogos).

Tips, ideas and activities

● Dialogic teaching involves every child in talking (and listening) about the subject under discussion. Whenever you ask a question of the class, expect them to turn to a 'talking partner' and come up with an answer between them. This means providing tasks that open their language up, rather than closed questions that shut language down (for some suggestions, see page 17).

● If the question is a tricky one, it helps to give children a few seconds of 'thinking time', during which everyone considers it silently before they begin discussion. Some children may want to make notes during this period, so ensure they have ready access to pencil and paper.

● Give a time limit for paired discussion, as appropriate to the topic. For instance, if it is a short, simple task like *Think of three adjectives to describe this character,* they probably will not need more than about 30 seconds. If you want them to struggle with a philosophical question, they will need longer! But gauge how the discussion is going – if they are all productively engaged, leave them to it rather than sticking to an arbitrary time limit.

● When you call the class together, pick a few children to feed back their discussion/ideas. Do not ask for 'hands up' volunteers – everyone has had a chance to talk, so everyone should have something to offer. Use the listening suggestions on the next page to acknowledge every contribution respectfully, even rather daft ones.

● After the class has listened to a few points of view, you could open it up for further contributions. This is the time when you can sensitively correct any wild misconceptions (*I'm not sure about the reasons we've got for Henry having Anne Boleyn beheaded. Does anyone have an alternative explanation?*).

You Can... Be a model listener

One of the most important ways children learn is through imitation. If you want them to listen actively and effectively, you must demonstrate good listening skills yourself.

Thinking points

- To listen actively to children, adults need:
  - generally, to respect the child as a speaker with something to say
  - specifically, to hear and understand exactly what the child is telling them (which may not always be immediately clear).

- You cannot listen actively if you think you have all the answers, or if you are only concerned about achieving a particular teaching objective. You have to keep an open mind. But if you do, you will often be very pleasantly surprised.

- There are many occasions for modelling good listening, such as:
  - circle time
  - listening to feedback in dialogic teaching
  - when questions arise during class discussion.

Tips, ideas and activities

- When you are listening to a child, demonstrate the social listening skills described on page 8. To listen actively, tune into the child completely – body language, facial expression, tone of voice and so on – and always respond with some genuine acknowledgement (*Gosh! I didn't know that!... That's really interesting – how do you know?... That's very sad.*).

- Children often struggle with ideas to start with, but given time and encouragement, they will get there. Try encouraging like:
  - *I'm not sure I understand yet. Can you explain?*
  - *Hmm – tell me more about that.*

- Do not fall into the habit of repeating everything every child says. If you are not absolutely clear as to the meaning, you might want to echo what you understand: *So you're saying that fireworks are dangerous and no one should be allowed to buy them?* But if you are genuinely teaching listening, children should be able to listen to each other – encourage them to face the class when speaking, and to speak up and speak out.

- If a child tries to buttonhole you when you are not able to listen, apologise politely: *I'm sorry, Fraser, but I don't have time to talk now.* However, if the conversation needs following up, make a note about it and let the child see you stick it on your bulletin board, to remind you to discuss it with them when time permits.

- On the other hand, if a child is slow to respond, resist the temptation to speed things up by answering or explaining yourself. And do not be afraid of silence. Children often need 'thinking time' to work out what they want to say. If you leap in to help them out, you will ruin their chance of finding their own words. Similarly, if there is a child who always answers, find ways to shush them. For example:
  - aim your questions at other children (and brook no interruptions)
  - be direct: *Let's give someone else a chance to answer, Ben. It's polite to give people thinking time.*

You Can... **Create a 'L

You Can... **Encourage children to talk**

All too often the way adults talk to children closes down their talk, rather than opening it up. In order to model listening, you need to ensure children have something interesting to tell you.

Thinking points

● During dialogic teaching or day to day conversation, most children are unlikely to speak in sentences, or be grammatically correct. When exploring and expressing ideas, they will probably use spoken language patterns (and lots of 'time-fillers' such as 'you know', 'like', 'sort of'). Do not worry about grammatical correctness in these circumstances. If a child has difficulty expressing something, you might repeat it back to them in sentence form, for them to confirm that you have understood, but do not expect them to parrot your sentence back – save *listen – imitate – innovate* for specific teaching situations.

● Many children decide early on not to bother contributing in class, because of the risk they will get a wrong answer and feel bad. If there are silent children in your class, make an extra effort to show them interest.

Tips, ideas and activities

● There are many occasions in the school day – in addition to dialogic teaching – when you will find yourself asking children questions. Try to avoid closed questions that expect a 'correct' answer. If the child knows the answer, he or she gives it and that is that. If the child does not know the answer, that is that again – and the child also feels bad. Three useful openers are:

○ *I wonder what/why/how…?*
○ *What/why/how do you think…?*
○ *Talk through your ideas about what/why/how…*

Or you could feign ignorance:

○ *I need help here! What do you suggest?*

● Similarly, if a child shows you some work, avoid the throwaway (*Oh, that's brilliant!*). Instead, make a genuine comment and try to open a dialogue: *I can see you've taken lots of trouble over this. Why have you used so much green over here…?* or: *This looks really interesting. Tell me about it.*

● If a child says something silly, do not put them down (see page 16). Assume it is you that is silly, because you cannot understand what they are getting at.

● There are more ideas in:
○ The *Talk To Me* handbook and whiteboard show (Basic Skills Agency, www.basic-skills.org.uk)
○ *How to Talk so Kids Will Listen and Listen so Kids Will Talk* by Adele Faber and Elaine Mazlish (Scribner).

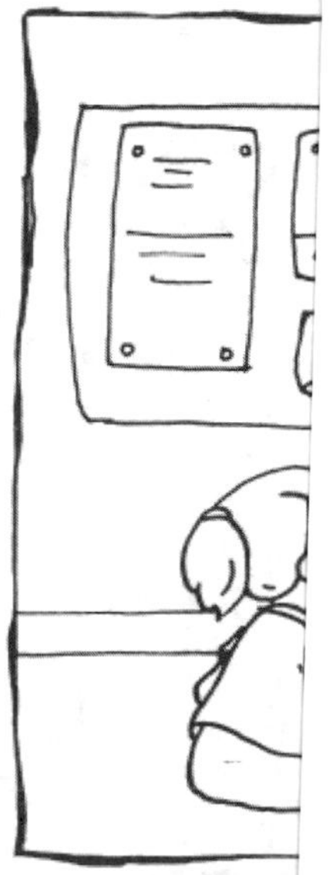

(left partially visible page)

You Can... U

Thinking po

● Until about 10 y
teachers could assu
most children, listen
develop naturally. C
automatically had th
experiences that un
and attention skills
and talked to as bal
around relatively fre
everyday domestic
with adults, playing
got older). Now ma
lead a sedentary, sc
existence, deprived
attention, so teach
aware of the factor
listening and atten

● As well as doing
works, stop doing
does not work! A t
told me that she h
boy with ADHD, 'V
never listen to wha
says?' 'I don't nee
'You'll tell me agai
anyway.'

You Can...

You Can... **Use explicit praise to encourage good listening**

When you are learning, it helps to know exactly when and how you are succeeding. You can help children along by explicitly praising evidence of good listening skills.

Thinking points

● These ideas of
suggestions, base
seen other teache
may have your ov
workable models.
important to invo
any decisions, for
on page 14. For o
assessment of chi
see page 55 and
page 62.

● Teachers very
opportunity to o
class. Other peop
(teaching assista
and may be able
insight, but teac
too deeply invol
watch what is ha
objectively. Yet i
sometimes just t
observe – espec
something like s
listening.

Thinking points

● All children crave attention and positive feedback, so praise is one of the most important tools available to a teacher. Children who are praised are usually anxious to repeat the behaviour. But with something as invisible as listening skills, your praise must be explicit or they will not know what to repeat.

● Praising individual children helps build your teaching rapport. So take particular trouble over children whom you find it difficult to praise. Look for any slight improvement, mentally work out why it is an improvement, and praise it! For instance, today can you say to any little monster: *Well done for staying still and looking at me while I said that?*

● Praise for a group helps bind that group together, further developing social skills.

Tips, ideas and activities

● When you see a child demonstrating a listening subskill, let them know that you are pleased and why, for example:

- *You're sitting so well today – managing to keep still and controlled – congratulations on your vestibular systems!*
- *I love the way you're making eye contact. It shows you're really tuning in to what ___ is saying.*
- *Excellent turn-taking! No one's interrupted and we're all concentrating on what the speaker says. Pats on the back all round!*
- *What a wonderful memory! You've remembered the words exactly. You must have listened very carefully to learn like that.*
- *How clever of you to listen and imagine so well. You've made a wonderful picture in your head. Who needs TV when you can make your own pictures?*
- *You could listen for Britain! You've managed to concentrate so well and for so long. I don't think any other children of your age could listen for so long.*
- *Well done! You listened carefully and imitated exactly what I said. Let's hear it again.*

● Praise children both individually and as groups. Try to find opportunities to praise children who have problems with listening. The minute you see any progress, explicitly praise it so the child is aware that he or she is moving forward.

You Can... **Keep noise levels down so everyone can listen**

Children cannot learn to listen in a noisy environment. It is up to the teacher to create a calm, quiet, purposeful ethos in the classroom so that listening is possible and enjoyable.

Thinking points

- If we want children to listen, they need a calm, quiet environment. But many teachers allow noise to increase to the level when they have to raise their own voices.

- If a child is fidgeting uncontrollably, he or she is unlikely to be listening, and is probably distracting others. If possible, give him or her a reason to leave the classroom for a while; for example, taking a message to another teacher (perhaps a note saying *Please give this child a book to carry back to me;* if you think they will read it, write in French), or, if your school grounds are secure, going for a short walk or run. When he or she returns, sit him or her down somewhere where he or she's less likely to cause disruption.

Tips, ideas and activities

- Start as you mean to go on. Make calm, quiet, purposeful activity your aim from Day One. If you inherit a rowdy class, it may be advisable to use suggestions from Chapter 1 to establish some basic attention and listening skills before embarking on a full-blown Listening Classroom strategy.

- Explain to the children that you run a calm classroom and discuss how they can help – as mentioned earlier, if they have ownership of the rules and routines, they are more likely to follow them. Help them recognise the levels of noise that are acceptable – such as a low buzz of conversation *'in quiet indoor voices'* – and congratulate children for appropriate behaviour, while clamping down immediately on loud shrieks, banging, etc. However, always model calm, quiet, purposeful behaviour yourself (let signs and symbols do your shouting for you – see page 46).

- Make sure there is a place where children *can* make a noise – boys especially do need to be able to escape from your calm haven sometimes. Access to an outdoor area is ideal, especially if some of it is shielded from the classroom so noise does not penetrate. Provide opportunities throughout the day for boisterous children to go out, run off energy and get noise out of their system – if possible, whenever they need it, not just at dedicated break times. If there is no escape, it will be difficult for them to keep buttoned up indoors.

- As your class gradually does become calm and quiet, congratulate them warmly. Let them know that you consider yourself lucky to teach such a wonderful group of people – probably the most receptive and well-behaved children in the developed world. Give them something to live up to.

- There are many more valuable suggestions in *You Can Create a Calm Classroom, 7–11* by Sue Cowley (Scholastic).

You Can... # Use circle activities to build listening stamina

Circle time is ideal for building listening stamina. In fact, unless you target this skill, many circle time activities can be ruined by children's inability to attend.

Thinking points

● If children have poor attention skills, circle time can become boring or chaotic. Those who have not yet had a turn or those who have already spoken lose interest and start fidgeting or misbehaving. In a large circle of 30 children, the teacher may spend all her time on crowd control, trying to keep sections of the circle on task. This is not only a waste of the teacher's time and energy, it is positively counter-productive because children are learning *not* to listen to each other.

● Some teachers are reluctant to work with a small group, thinking that the rest of the class might misbehave. If, however, by working with small groups, you develop children's listening and attention skills, there should be much less mischief in the future.

Tips, ideas and activities

● Do not expect children with attention problems to be able to listen for more than a couple of minutes to begin with. Try this introductory circle time on the first day of term – just you and, say, six to eight children:

○ Demonstrate how to make eye contact with the person beside you and introduce yourself, for example: *Hello, my name is Mrs Palmer and I teach at Comiston Primary School, Oxgangs Road, Edinburgh EH13 2TD.*

○ Each child then makes eye contact and introduces him or herself to the next person, repeating the formula but substituting their own name and address, hobby or fact about themselves.

○ Praise the children individually for their performance, especially the way they listen when not actually personally involved.

Repeat this activity with all the children in small groups, while the rest of the class get on with some work or have free time.

● Make a note of those children who have difficulty attending, so that the next day you can adjust the size of the circle:

○ children who found it difficult remain in a smaller group

○ those who found it easy to attend and participate join a larger group (which will take longer).

● Do short circle times every day for a week or so until the majority of the class is able to function in one or two large circles. Children who are still experiencing difficulty need extra help – and this is well worth an investment of time and teaching. See Lucky Duck publications (www.luckyduck.co.uk) for ideas.

● Once you feel the listening habit is established in most children, make your circle times less frequent but longer.

You Can... **Use circle activities to teach social listening**

Circle time is all about social listening. It is the perfect place to rehearse and revise social skills you want children to use throughout the school day.

Thinking points

● Do not feel you have to provide different activities for each circle time. Remember the importance of repetition in young children's learning. You can use a quick activity like passing a look round the circle many times, but it helps to make slight variations (as suggested opposite) to keep the children interested.

● Circle time thus combines Personal, Social and Emotional education with speaking and listening, and the opportunity to link to other curricular areas, particularly in terms of introducing new vocabulary and language structures.

Tips, ideas and activities

● You can use circle time as an opportunity to home in on all the social listening skills. For instance, one of the best ways to help children make eye contact is to 'pass a look around the circle'. This could be a regular opening for your circle time, ringing the changes by:
  ● turning it into a wink, a smile or a compliment
  ● suggesting particular facial expressions (happy, sad, shocked, proud, and so on).
The circle activity on page 22 can also be used as an opening gambit on other occasions, with children giving other information about themselves, such as date and place of birth, favourite school subjects and so on.

● Circle time is an ideal opportunity to model active listening, and to convey to children that good listening is as important as good talking. Make sure the children are very clear about rules (use visual cue cards to remind them when they forget – see pages 46 and photocopiable page 61), and make sure your circle is the right size.

● There are many suggestions for activities at various levels in:
  ● the Lucky Duck catalogue (www.luckyduck.co.uk)
  ● Jenny Moseley's Quality Circle Time materials (www.circle-time.co.uk).

You Can... Use circle time to develop imaging skills

There are many reasons to encourage children to 'see pictures in their heads' in circle time, and they tend to be quiet, restful activities – ideal for developing a range of listening skills.

Thinking points

● Mental imaging is an established technique for stress-management, so highly relevant to the PSE function of circle time. Many children today lead fairly frantic, chaotic lives, so it can be helpful to them to have safe or calm places to retreat to if necessary in their heads. Once they have acquired the technique, some teachers might be able to integrate it into strategies for anger management or conflict resolution.

● These activities require a quiet environment, so if only part of the class is in the circle, you will have to find somewhere to take them away from distractions – or use a time when the other half are perhaps playing outdoors.

Tips, ideas and activities

● Use circle time for asking children to use their imaginations. Make sure they are sitting comfortably on a chair, then ask them to close their eyes and imagine that it is the end of the school day: *You're feeling very tired and you just want to get home and have a rest. Think about a special place in your house where you'll go to relax.* Give them a few moments to decide, then: *In your head, imagine yourself going through the door into your house and going to your special place. Can you see it? Settle down in your special place and feel all cosy. Think about what you can see around you. What can you hear? What can you smell? What you can feel against your skin?* Finally, ask the children to open their eyes and go round the circle, saying a couple of sentences about their special place. You model it first, for example: *My special place at home is my sofa. It's red with big, soft cushions. I like to snuggle there with my dog.*

● On another occasion, find a piece of restful music (such as Grieg's *Morning* or Saint-Saens' *The Swan*). Ask the children to think of lovely, quiet places they would like to visit when they are angry or frightened – a beach, woodland, a beautiful room – somewhere safe, calm and restful. Go round the circle asking for suggestions. Then ask children to think of a special place for themselves, close their eyes and, when the music starts, imagine themselves in their calm place. Play the music for as long as appropriate for their level of listening stamina – do not let them get restless. Try to create a magical, restful feeling. In another circle time, let the children revisit their calm place. You could then use the music on occasions when you want to calm the class, or create a quiet atmosphere.

● There are many visualisation activities you can adapt from *Circle Time Activities for Relaxation and Imagination* by Tony Pryce (Lucky Duck Publishing).

You Can... **Use circle time to develop literate language**

Circle time is a great opportunity for using the listen – imitate – innovate *technique to familiarise children with the rhythms and patterns of written language.*

Thinking points

● For many children, structured opportunities such as these may be the only times they actually speak in complete sentences. It is therefore essential to recognise the importance of the *listen – imitate – innovate* model in underpinning children's success as writers, and finding ways to integrate it into teaching across the curriculum.

Tips, ideas and activities

● Circle time provides an opportunity for using the *listen – imitate – innovate* technique (see page 13) to familiarise children with the rhythms and patterns of written language. Indeed, it is an excellent context to introduce children to the concept of 'a sentence' gradually without any explicit teaching. Whenever you intend to use a sentence frame, introduce the session with the words, *We're going to say a sentence today.* This allows children to hear the term 'sentence' within a meaningful context, and is much more likely to help them understand the concept over time than a decontexualised explanation such as, *A sentence makes complete sense.*

● The younger the children, the shorter the sentence you should use. Say the beginning of the sentence, adding your particular ending, for instance: *My favourite time at school is… circle time.* Ensure the first few children to speak after you have good auditory memories so they will give a good, clear rendition. As the sentence frame goes round the circle, the less able children will hear it repeated many times and will have a better chance of internalising the frame. After *listening*, they have the option of *imitating* or *innovating*, for example: *My favourite time at school is break.*

● With older children, you can use more complex sentence constructions, such as:
My favourite time at school is… because…
When I get home, the first thing I do is…
If I feel sad, I like to…

● If there is a particular sort of construction you want children to be aware of, you can introduce it through circle time. For instance, in the later years of primary school, children need to start varying the types of causal language they use in written explanations. So instead of *My favourite time at school is… because…*, on different days, give alternative constructions:
My favourite time at school is circle time. The reason is that… This is because… I like… Consequently, my favourite time at school is circle time.

● You can find selections of key language structures in *Speaking Frames* (see page 13).

You Can... Develop children's ability to keep a steady beat

The ability to keep a steady beat is essential to listening and learning, so activities that develop beat competence should be part of any course in listening skills.

Thinking points

- Research has shown that one of the most significant indicators of children's success at school is the ability to keep a steady beat. It is clearly connected with:
  - bodily coordination and control
  - the patterning of information in the brain
  - overall listening skills.
Auditory memory depends to a large extent on beat competence: think of the way we use beat in counting, in reciting the alphabet, the months of the year, and so on.

- All the activities in this section on music, movement and song should help develop beat competence. A teacher in Finland, where music and song are threaded throughout the school day, explained that 'Music trains the mind to pattern and the ears to sound.' Both very important for listening!

Tips, ideas and activities

- With younger children, introduce:
  - 'Copycat': You model a simple beat (for example, clap your hands twice, tap knees twice, and so on) and ask children as a group to copy you. Gradually introduce slightly more complex rhythms (for example, clappety-clap, clappety-clap, clappety-clappety-clappety-clap). When the group is good at it, ask individual children to model sequences.
  - 'Chopsticks': Give each child a paper plate and a chopstick, and sit them in a circle. Ask one child to use the chopstick to tap a simple rhythm on the plate, then get the others to copy it. Develop 'chopstick conversations' where one child (or half the group) taps out a rhythm, and another child (or the other half of the group) taps a 'reply'.

- Use raps for teaching, such as the 'Punctuation Street Rap' on photocopiable page 56. Encourage the children to make up simple raps featuring information learned across the curriculum (such as the Water Cycle Rap). Get the class performing these with plenty of body movement, clapping, etc.

- Encourage clapping games and rhymes. These are excellent for coordination skills, and many include cross-over movements that help make connections between the two sides of the brain. There are many examples in Jenny Mosley's book *Clapping Games* (Positive Press), and in 'The Spelling Song' on photocopiable page 57 you can use a mixture of clapping (with words) and high-fives (with the 'yeahs' in the chorus).

- Encourage children to learn to skip and to chant skipping rhymes, such as: *Salt, mustard, vinegar, pepper* or the old cherry-counting chant: *Tinker, tailor, soldier, sailor, rich man, poor man, beggarman, thief.*

- Almost every musical activity (especially dancing and marching – see page 27) involves a steady beat. Encourage children's awareness by clapping, foot tapping and making other rhythmic movements yourself when teaching them.

You Can... **Develop coordination through musical activities**

Blending words, rhythm, music and actions helps children develop bodily control, balance and attention span.

Thinking points

● Children need strong connections between the left hemisphere of the brain (where the brain processes words, linear sequences and pattern) and the right (specialising in holistic patterning, spatial awareness and music). Action songs, marching songs, clapping and skipping rhymes are all great – and natural – ways of promoting connections between the hemispheres.

● In the past, music, dance and song were common activities in primary schools, but in recent years, there has been a tendency to concentrate instead on more academic approaches. However, now that listening skills are not developing naturally, this sort of productive fun is more essential than ever.

Tips, ideas and activities

● Moving to music is a great way to develop control. Patterned rhythmic music helps children pattern their body movement, and moving to music with others helps develop social skills. Start each day with a short aerobics session, using funky music that the children enjoy, and letting them help you devise simple actions.

● In preparation for Christmas parties each year, teach country dances (for example, *Sir Roger de Coverley*, *Strip the Willow*, *Gay Gordons*, *Eightsome Reels*). Older pupils influenced by the current 'culture of cool' may be resistant to this sort of dancing initially, so the trick is to introduce them for the Year 3 (Scottish Primary 4) party, and then carry them through each succeeding year.

● Use marching as an activity in PE. Play some stirring marching music, and let the children move to it freely. Then show them how to march in step and devise some marching routines, for example:

- children march in single file from A to B, then peel off to alternate sides, and march back to A
  - having met up with a partner coming from the opposite side, they now march in twos from A to B, and peel off in twos
  - on return to A, the twos form into fours… etc.

This can take some time to teach, but is great fun and most children enjoy it – they can associate it with soldierly behaviour or being cheerleaders.

● Teach children rousing marching songs like *Pack up Your Troubles in Your Old Kit Bag* and encourage them to sing while marching in the playground, on outdoor trips, etc.

You Can... Use music and song to develop children's social listening

Singing or moving to music as a group helps children literally to work in harmony. It means they attend to the sound made by the whole group, not just themselves.

Thinking points

● Since time immemorial, human beings have used music, rhythm and song to socialise their young. Until very recently, for instance, every school day began with a 'corporate act of worship', when the whole school gathered and belted out a couple of hymns together. In schools in many parts of the world, they sing the National Anthem first thing in the morning, starting each day with a communal commitment to citizenship. There is an essential human need that music fulfils.

● There are examples of the team-building uses of song throughout history – think of the sea-shanties that helped sailors pull together, working songs that helped labourers in the fields, and soldiers' marching songs.

Tips, ideas and activities

● Starting the day with an aerobics session, as suggested on page 27, is not just good for developing physical coordination and control – it also has a socialising effect. If children start the day by listening and moving in concert with others, they are likely to be more disposed to listen and act as a team when formal schoolwork begins.

● Another way to help children pull together is to get them singing as a group. On later pages, I recommend the power of song for developing a range of listening skills, which means you will need regular singing sessions. Make use of these for socialising purposes, to help children who find it difficult to maintain attention as part of the group. Call the class together for a sing-song:
  ● to settle them back into class after a break
  ● if they are restless (for example, children are often very edgy and uncontrolled during windy, stormy weather)
  ● if you are unhappy with the atmosphere in class.

● Do not worry if you are not much of a singer yourself. The main quality required in terms of your voice is gusto. (And as the possessor of a singularly awful singing voice, I can vouch for the fact that children are very forgiving.) But it is essential that you – and, indeed, all adults in the classroom – join in.

● As children become proficient at singing, create 'conversations' by splitting the class in half and giving each half a section to sing. Start with simple echoing songs such as *Frère Jacques*, and then try singing it as a round. Folk songs like *The Lincolnshire Poacher* or *Green Grow the Rushes Oh* are designed to be sung as conversations.

● Marching (see page 27) is a teambuilding exercise, involving moving in concert with other people. This is one of the reasons the armed forces place so much store by marching – it helps forge a sense of belonging to the group. So do simple folk dances – they are highly collaborative, and the constant repetition helps lay down strong neural networks upon which future collaborative endeavours can be built.

You Can... Use music to develop sound discrimination

Music-making of all kinds develops children's appreciation of and capacity to discriminate between sounds.

Thinking points

● Music is the obvious vehicle for developing listening skills of all kinds, but particularly discriminative listening. Children's own experimentation is the best way to develop an interest in sounds.

● Making music involves remembering sequences of sounds, which is an important aspect of auditory memory, especially in literacy. For instance, phonic decoding involves remembering sequences of phonemes, starting with short consonant–vowel–consonant sequences (for example, c-a-t), but building up longer ones (for example, c-r-u-n-ch). Later, when spelling, they will need to hold sequences of syllables in their heads (for example, mul-ti-syll-ab-ic).

Tips, ideas and activities

● As well as your timetabled music lessons, look for every opportunity to bring music into the children's lives. Take them to concerts, invite pupils who are learning musical instruments to stage concerts in school, play soft music as a background for quiet study, and rousing music when children need to be motivated.

● Look for opportunities to use music as part of your teaching. For instance, when teaching punctuation, ask children to choose musical sounds to represent the various punctuation marks. Discuss the best sound for each mark, drawing their attention to the significance of pitch, volume, length of sound, etc. When you have decided on your 'musical punctuation', give groups of children a piece of prose to read to the class, with musical accompaniment each time there is a punctuation mark. (One class I tried this with actually tried taking out the words and just playing the punctuation – and we got rather a nice tune!)

● Use instruments for this memory game. You need two sets of the same small instruments (for example, drum, rattle, triangle, shaker, chime bar).
  ○ Put one set in front of a screen of some kind and the other behind it.
  ○ Using the instruments *behind* the screen, play a sequence of sounds, placing the instruments down in sequence as you do so (start with two, and build up as children become more skilful). Remove any unused instruments.
  ○ Now ask children to identify the instruments they heard and place them in front of the screen in the correct sequence.
  ○ Then remove the screen. The children will have immediate feedback about the accuracy of their choice. Talk about any wrong choices and why they might have happened.

● Encourage children to use instruments to make up their own short musical sequences for use as classroom jingles or themes.

You Can... Improve auditory memory through song

Songs are an excellent vehicle for developing auditory memory because they are fun to repeat. Children enjoy the sounds of the patterned language, the feeling of the rhythm and the satisfaction of acquisition.

Thinking points

● The secret of auditory memory is repetition, repetition, repetition, especially the repetition of sequences of words, rhythm and actions. Once children have memorised a song or rhyme, they enjoy singing or reciting it, so repetition happens naturally – this helps set down strong neural networks that will stand them in good stead for further auditory memory work. Treat auditory memory as a kind of mental muscle that needs constant exercising to become strong and efficient.

● The communal nature of sing-songs is particularly helpful for children with poor listening skills. To start with, the children with good auditory memories carry them along. Gradually, as the words become more familiar, everyone begins to remember them.

Tips, Ideas and activities

● Build up a repertoire of songs and chants that your class learns to sing by heart and without accompaniment. This could include:

- alphabet and tables songs or chants
- songs made up by yourself and/or the children to teach particular facts (for instance, see my 'Spelling Song' and 'Sentence Song' on photocopiable page 57)
- traditional and folk songs (particularly ones from your local area)
- 'camp-fire' and music hall songs
- seasonal songs, such as carols at Christmas, harvest songs
- favourites suggested by the children.

Action songs, combining kinaesthetic with auditory memory, are particularly powerful. If a song does not have actions, you (or the children) could make up your own.

● When you introduce a song, you may want some musical accompaniment to help children learn the tune. Music publishers like A&C Black often include CDs with their publications, and many simple tunes for folk songs and so on are now available on the internet.

● To teach the words of a song by heart, write them up on the whiteboard for the children to read as they sing it through a couple of times. Then, each time you sing, rub out a few of the words, leaving spaces where they used to be, so pupils have to remember more and more of it. Start by rubbing out fairly obvious words (such as rhyming words), and gauge how much you can lose at a time to create just the right amount of challenge.

● Provide photocopied song sheets for children to take home so parents can join in too (see photocopiable page 59 – 'Letter to parents').

● Perhaps you and the class could compose a special class song, to help forge a sense of group identity and pride.

You Can... Use music to develop mental imaging

Listening to music can help all of us conjure up moods and pictures. Let children respond to music through movement, talk, art and writing in order to develop the capacity to 'see pictures in their heads.'

Thinking points

● Many modern children have the same problem with creating mental images to go with music as they do with words. If you help them use movement as a vehicle for developing mental imagery, they have the added power of the kinaesthetic learning channel.

Tips, ideas and activities

● Make a collection of 'programme' music that tells stories or paints pictures – happy, sad, wild, serene, clumsy, graceful. Well-known programme music popular with children includes *Peter and the Wolf*, *The Carnival of the Animals*, *The Planet Suite*, *Peer Gynt*, *1812 Overture* and most ballet music.

● With younger children, encourage moving to music, conveying how it makes them feel. For instance, you could play extracts from two contrasting pieces, such as Grieg's *Morning* and *The Hall of the Mountain King*. Ask them why the different music made them feel and move differently and ask: *What sort of pictures do these tunes conjure up?* Do not expect them to come up with the 'correct' pictures – let their imaginations have free rein. At the end of the session, you might tell them the titles of the pieces and the images the composer was trying to conjure, and let them listen one last time to see if they think he achieved it.

● With an older class, ask them to listen to a piece of music (for example, the opening section of Beethoven's *Fifth Symphony*) and come up with a story that fits the sounds. Then put them in groups to act out/mime their story as they listen to the music.

● Use music also as a stimulus for artwork, asking children to draw or paint to convey the pictures in their head.

● Use restful, gentle music alongside circle time imaging activities (see page 24), to help children conjure their own special world. If a certain tune becomes associated with this sort of calming activity, you might find it helpful as a way of calming the class when disruption has made them fractious.

● When children are proficient writers, use music as a stimulus for writing poems or short prose passages, changing the musical patterns into thoughts on paper.

You Can... Develop listening stamina with songs and rhymes

Singing favourite songs or listening to favourite tunes over and over again helps develop listening stamina and increase children's attention span.

Thinking points

● To adults, repetition is boring – we constantly seek variety and innovation. But for children – especially young or immature children – it is essential for the creation of strong neural networks, into which further learning can be slotted.

● Most parents in the past had a fairly limited repertoire, which was actually an advantage as it meant more of the repetition their children needed. But adults raised in a multimedia world crave variety, and assume that children do too. DVDs, videos, websites, and so on, provide that variety. But the result is less repetition, and less robust neural networks in children's brains.

● If we want to raise children's boredom threshold, develop listening stamina and improve attention span, we have to leap on every opportunity for enjoyable repetition of songs and rhymes at school.

Tips, ideas and activities

● Most primary school children enjoy singing cumulative or nonsense songs involving lots of repetition, such as:

- *Ten Green Bottles*
- *The Quartermaster's Store*
- *One Man Went to Mow*
- *The Animals Went in Two by Two*
- *Green Grow the Rushes Oh.*

You will probably find that they will happily go on singing such songs long after you have lost interest! They also enjoy songs like *The Bear Went Over the Mountain* that just go on and on and on… Grit your teeth, and let them sing! You can make use of their enthusiasm to fill in time on long bus journeys or when the class is obliged to wait around for any reason.

● Familiarity improves attention skills in terms of music too. If you want children to listen to and enjoy a piece of music, arrange for them to hear it several times before actually 'introducing' it. For instance, you could play it in the background as they arrive in the morning or are getting ready for home-time. Then, when it is well embedded, talk to them about it and invite them actually to listen – perhaps for a purpose such as imaging or artwork, or perhaps just for the pleasure of active listening. The more they have been exposed to the music beforehand, the longer they will be able to sit and concentrate on it.

You Can... # Target listening through reading aloud

Children love being read to – there is a natural craving in young human beings to hear stories. So reading aloud is a great vehicle for honing their listening skills on a daily basis and tuning their ears to the patterns of written language.

Thinking points

● Parents and teachers who do make the time and effort to read to children tend to stop round about the age of eight or nine, when the children have begun to read for themselves. But reading aloud is not just about access to books, it is about access to the sounds of literate language. As Robert Louis Stevenson said, we should always read to children, for how else will they learn 'the chime of fair words, and the march of the stately period?'

● Some teachers just read short stories or picture books. While there is a place for these, there should also be opportunities for children to share serialised full-length novels – listening to a serial involves auditory memory, and more complex mental imaging. It also builds listening stamina.

Tips, ideas and activities

● Read to children every day. Choose a book you personally enjoy and that you think will appeal to your class, especially the boys. Set aside 15–20 minutes of each day – perhaps immediately after lunch or before home-time – and read your 'class novel' as a serial. You might also find other odd times during the week when you can fit in a little extra reading.

● Do not feel guilty about spending time on reading aloud. Not only are you developing a wide range of listening skills (active listening, mental imaging, the building of listening stamina and the acquisition of literate language patterns), you are also introducing children to the enormous pleasure of sharing a good book.

● For this reason, do not use your class novel for too many 'literacy activities' – the more you associate it with work, the less fun it will be. There may be the odd occasion when it provides a useful example for something you are teaching in literacy lessons, but on the whole, keep it sacrosanct. Make 'class novel time' something for everyone to look forward to – a restful, relaxing period in the class's day.

● If possible, create a comfortable, cosy area where children can sit around to listen. (I positioned three tables to create a snug 'Story Space' in one corner of my classroom. This allowed tiers: some children sitting on the tables, others on chairs, a few on the floor. At other times, the tables could be used for group or individual work.)

● Make sure that, once you have read a book, there are copies available for children to read themselves. Make other books by that author available as well.

You Can... **Hone children's ear for language through reading**

In recent years, children have seldom been encouraged to read aloud. But for many, it is an important opportunity to develop an ear for literate language patterns and standard English grammar.

Thinking points

● The introduction of guided reading has led to a serious reduction in opportunities for children to read aloud. While there are many advantages to guided reading, in terms of developing children's reading strategies and critical faculties, there is also a strong case for reading aloud.

● As one whose early language was influenced by a dialect-speaking grandmother, I remember how alien 'school English' sounded during my early primary years. I also remember the feeling of strangeness when, reading aloud from my reading book, I said 'We were…' instead of the Lancastrian 'We was…' But these opportunities to mimic standard English gave me access to an alternative code of speech, necessary for success in the educational system.

Tips, ideas and activities

● Make sure children have plenty of opportunities to read aloud at their own level. This allows them:
- to hear the patterns of written language produced from their own mouths
- to know how standard English and literate vocabulary *feels*
- to respond physically to the ebb and flow of well-constructed sentences
- to learn from experience how punctuation guides meaning and expression.

This is particularly important for children who have English as an additional language and those who, because of home background, do not naturally speak standard English.

● Paired reading ensures plenty of opportunities for all children to read aloud. Ask children in pairs to choose and share the reading of a children's fiction book (at an appropriate reading age). Depending on age and ability, they might read alternate pages or alternate paragraphs: where there is a lot of dialogue, they may sometimes choose to read it like a play. Paired reading (in 'quiet indoor voices') is an ideal activity for keeping the rest of the class productively engaged while you are working with a group, so it works well alongside guided reading.

● You can also use paired reading when there is a piece of text you want the whole class to share (for instance, a piece of historical writing or a newspaper article). In this case, it may be better to pair able readers with poorer ones, so they can help with difficult words.

● While competent readers can read to each other, children with reading difficulties really need to read aloud as often as possible to an adult – yourself, a teaching assistant or perhaps a parent helper.

You Can... **Use poetry to develop listening skills**

Poetry arose as part of our oral tradition – positioned halfway between story and song – and so provides many opportunities for developing listening skills.

Thinking points

• Like music and song, poetry trains the mind to pattern and the ear to sound. While couched in poetic rather than literate language, it nevertheless introduces children's ears to cadences and rhythms that will be useful when they come to write.

• Like music, poetry is an immensely civilising force. Many teachers are wary about introducing poems to children, thinking they will find the language too challenging. But children are used to understanding only a fraction of the words adults use, and are very responsive to rhythm, tunes and emotion. If you try using poems with them, you will probably be pleasantly surprised.

Tips, ideas and activities

• Poetry is written to be heard – like song, it is intended to enter our heads through our ears, and its rhythmic, patterned language echoes there. It is therefore an ideal way of introducing new and vibrant vocabulary. As well as studying poems in literacy lessons, ensure children have plenty of opportunities to hear poems and read them aloud themselves.

• Start a tradition of 'Poem of the Week', which you revisit each day – it should not take more than five minutes, and could build up a repertoire of poems with which the class is familiar. Choose a poem related to the season or the weather, or to some area of study, or just one you like or think the children will find fun. Ring the changes in mood (sad, dramatic, inspirational, funny).

• Ring the changes also in the way you tackle it, for example:
  ◦ Monday: just read the poem to the class, allow a couple of minutes for talking partners to discuss it, and ask what they think.
  ◦ Tuesday: give out copies for them to follow as you read (any new thoughts from the talking partners?).
  ◦ Wednesday: two or more children, depending on the poem, present their rendition (see page 37 for ideas).
  ◦ Thursday: whole-class reading, in chorus.
  ◦ Friday: a final read through (you? a volunteer?), and the poem is ceremonially placed in the class's 'Poem of the Week' book.
If the poem is quite short, by this time quite a few of the class will probably know it by heart.

• If you are uneasy about reading poetry aloud yourself, make use of DVDs and tapes. After listening to other people reciting for a while, you will probably begin to feel inclined to have a go.

You Can... Encourage children to learn by heart and declaim poetry

The rhythm, rhyme and patterned language of poetry make it easy to learn by heart. This not only develops auditory memory – but also provides the learner with a treasure trove of verse to carry around in his or her head.

Thinking points

• In recent years, in our rush to teach poems as objects of academic study, we have often forgotten the sheer pleasure of reciting and listening to them. Much of the joy of poetry comes from repeated exposure, and often, a poet's message sinks in gradually over time.

• The healthy development of the brain is based in repetition – for children, familiarity encourages security, stability and strong neural networks. The repetition of poems (and songs) ensures that this strength includes auditory learning channels.

Tips, ideas and activities

• Frequent repetition of a 'Poem of the Week' (see page 35) will probably lead to some children learning several by heart. But every so often, ensure that the whole class learns a poem. Tackle the teaching in the same way as you would teach a song:

  • write the poem on the whiteboard for pupils to read and recite in chorus
  • gradually rub out words and phrases, so they are reciting more and more from memory.

This is the basic system underpinning the CD, *Learn By Heart: Around the Year* by Sue Palmer (Fosbury Enterprises) – listening and learning activities around poems, rhymes and jingles associated with the months and seasons.

• Once children have learned poems, give plenty of opportunities for 'declaiming', to help consolidate them in long-term memory. You could add group poetry recitals into your regular 'sing-songs' (see page 30), or go through your poetry repertoire when waiting for the bell, on the bus, etc. You could also invite volunteers to recite their favourites (see below).

• Older children who have already had experience of learning by heart should be allowed to choose their own poems to learn. When I was eleven, our teacher challenged us all to commit a long narrative poem to heart, learning it in stages over the course of the year. I learned *The Lady of Shallott*, and have been glad of her company at bus stops for well over 40 years.

• Try allocating a certain time of the week as a 'Performance Space' where children with a poem to declaim, an instrument to play, a song to sing, and so on, can enjoy their moment in the sun performing to the group. As well as the boost to the performers' auditory memory, this gives the whole class an opportunity for focused sustained listening.

You Can... **Encourage listening through performance**

It is fun to play with sound when staging readings, recitation and performances, and this provides opportunities for children to listen discriminatively.

Thinking points

● This activity links poetry and prose to drama, music and *play* – one of the most vital ingredients in children's learning. The younger the child, the more play is personal and unstructured, and the more he or she learns from it. As children grow older, they increasingly seek structured play – team and board games, sporting activities and performance. But they still learn from it, alongside more formal methods.

● In adulthood, play for most of us is relegated to our spare time (we play the piano, football, chess, poker, and so on, or go to see other people play in sporting events or performing in plays). Unless you are David Beckham or Tom Cruise, play will not earn you money, so we undervalue it and forget how vital it is to our Children.

Tips, ideas and activities

● When studying or learning poems, show the class how to enhance performance by using a variety of:
  ● voices (female/male; old/young; solo/chorus; large/small group)
  ● voice tone, volume, pitch, speed of delivery
  ● sound effects
  ● (if appropriate) musical accompaniment.

Encourage groups of children to use these techniques in their own performances for the class.

● Making sound effects is great for tuning children's ears to sound. They do not need any special equipment. For instance, they could use:
  ● paper cups and plates for tapping, banging or rubbing together
  ● paper of various kinds for crackling, tearing, flapping
  ● corrugated paper and a pencil for a washboard effect
  ● Brio cubes for banging together
  ● metal, plastic or glass containers and a pencil for tapping and banging.

● Do not just stick to poems. Introduce your class to Readers' Theatre, a popular strategy in the States (see, for example, www.readerstheatre.com). Give groups of children a short piece of poetry or prose to dramatise and perform for the rest of the class, using the techniques above.

● As well as using them in your regular 'Performance Space' (see page 36), you could present these productions for other classes or parents, or record them on video or audio for children to watch (and listen to) critically.

You Can... Develop listening and presentation skills together

Dictation is a means of focusing on word and sentence level skills through listening.

Thinking points

● Dictation, used with discretion, can be a very useful resource in a teacher's repertoire, and is a good way of developing listening and presentational skills. But, while a little dictation now and again can be helpful, too much is a recipe for dreary teaching.

● It is important to build up listening stamina for dictation, starting with a short sentence or two and gradually increasing the length. But five or ten minutes is more than enough for anyone.

Tips, ideas and activities

● Writing from dictation lets children concentrate on presentation skills (handwriting, spelling, punctuation) without the distraction of simultaneously considering what to write and composing it into sentences.

● It is particularly useful as a way of revising/assessing spelling. You integrate some of the spelling words children have recently learned into a short dictation passage – this provides an opportunity to write the words in context. (Some teachers ask children to learn the spellings and use the words in a story for homework; then they choose the best story and tidy it up to be the week's dictation.)

● When dictating, follow this routine:
  ○ read the whole passage through so the children are familiar with the overall context
  ○ read it section by section, pausing between chunks to give the children time to write
  ○ at the end, read through it again slowly so they can check their writing and fill in any missing bits.

● Indicate the punctuation as you read, to provide an auditory echo of where punctuation should occur. You could use
  ○ a different tone of voice, for example:
  CAPITAL LETTER She came into the room FULL STOP...
  OPEN SPEECH MARKS, CAPITAL LETTER: Hello COMMA, CLOSE SPEECH MARKS... she said FULL STOP...
  ○ the musical punctuation technique described on page 29:
  DRRRRR! She came into the room DONG! SQUEAK DRRRRRR! Hello TING! SQUEAK DRRRRR! ... she said DONG!

You Can... **Use mental imaging to enhance creative writing**

Children who are not used to 'making pictures in their heads' often find it difficult to write imaginatively and creatively. This strategy, from Birmingham teacher Sarah Bott, helps them draw on mental imagery.

Thinking points
- Children who are used to watching 'stories on screen' are often unaware of the significance of background detail to a story. They have been spoon-fed with images and sound effects, and have not recognised the contribution these make to the atmosphere and mood. Sarah Bott's technique is a sort of 'mental drama' activity, which increases awareness of the way all our senses contribute to the evocation of a scene.

Tips, ideas and activities
- Choose a few children with good imaginative powers to help you demonstrate the method. Bring them to the front of the class and give each of them a pair of goggles or spectacles to wear. Explain that these are 'Virtual Reality Goggles', and that when they put them on, they will be transported to a virtual world.

- After giving the instruction: *Goggles on!* tell them whereabouts they are, for example: *You are now at the seaside!* Ask them questions and encourage them to call out answers. For instance:
  - *What can you see?* (sand, children playing, the sea, blue sky…)
  - *What can you hear?* (seagulls screaming, children's voices, the waves crashing…)
  - *What can you feel?* (the sand in my toes, the sun on my back…).

- Use these answers in a piece of shared writing, for example: James stood on the sandy beach, looking out to sea. *Before him, two children were building a castle, and their excited voices cut into his thoughts. Seagulls wheeled above, slicing the blue sky with their cries. He could feel the gritty sand between his toes, the hot sun on his back.*

- Explain to the class that Virtual Reality Goggles help writers get the feel of an environment, so they can bring it to life on the page. As it is not possible to provide glasses/goggles for everyone, ask the class to work out a symbolic way of putting 'Goggles on!', such as holding their fists in front of their closed eyes.

- Use the technique to help them 'brainstorm' through mental imaging before beginning to write. For the first few times, call out the cues given above. Once children have got the idea, expect them to put 'Goggles on!' and transport themselves.

You Can... Use storytelling to develop listening skills

Since time immemorial, adults have taught children how to listen by telling them stories. Pie Corbett has devised a way of using this age-old technique to develop auditory memory and prepare children to write their own stories.

Thinking points

● Over a school year, you could teach children five or six stories in this way. As well as developing their language and listening skills, you are filling their heads with characters, settings and plots – and ways to express them – that they can use to write stories for themselves.

● The technique makes use of the two key learning strategies of imitation and repetition, while the use of actions and story-maps supports learning through visual and kinaesthetic channels.

● For more information and many other good ideas, see Pie Corbett's *Bumper Book of Storytelling into Writing Key Stage 2* (Clown Publishing – available on Amazon).

Tips, ideas and activities

● Pie Corbett has used this technique throughout the primary school, but I have found it particularly effective at the lower end of the junior school (when children are seven or eight and just getting into writing stories).

● Choose a repetitive folk tale you know well, such as:
'The Three Little Pigs'
'The Gingerbread Man'
'The Three Billy Goats Gruff'
'The Little Red Hen'
'The Enormous Turnip'
or adapt a fable, myth or legend to tell as a story.

● Work out your own version of the story, including devising actions to accompany it. Then practise telling your story (with the actions) a few times until you feel fluent. Make a picture 'story-map' showing the main events of the story in sequence (this does not have to be grand – stick figures and rough squiggles are actually better than a smart visual representation).

● Tell the story, with actions, to the class. Then repeat it, a line at a time, asking the children to imitate you (both words and actions). Display your story-map, so children have an overview of the whole thing, and then tell the whole story again, asking the children to join in.

● Tell the story a couple of times every day, aiming for them to learn it by heart within a few days. After several practices, take away your story-map and ask the children to make their own. Once they have a reasonable grasp of the story, get them to practise in pairs, facing each other, as well as in the whole group. Ask some of the word-perfect children to take over your place and lead the group.

You Can... **Use storytelling to develop literate language**

Storytelling is like a bridge between spoken and written language. Pie Corbett uses it to familiarise children with sentence structures and useful written vocabulary, such as connectives.

Thinking points

● If you read aloud to children, they will hear many useful written language patterns, but your own storytelling is an opportunity to target specific useful words and language structures. Choose the sort of words, phrases and sentence frames you want children to use in their own writing in the future.

● As evidence of pupil progress, try Pie Corbett's method of assessment. He simply selects three children before he starts (an able, middle-ability and lower-ability child) and asks them to tell a story into a tape-recorder. Then he repeats the procedure at the end. The difference in language ability and confidence, especially for middle- and lower-ability pupils, is startling.

Tips, ideas and activities

● As well as using stories to develop auditory memory, you can use storytelling to introduce some of the language features children need in their *writing*. If they learn these language features orally first, they will have them as auditory echoes in their heads when they come to write.

● Think of your story as having four distinct parts, each with certain key language features:
  ● **introduction**, giving essential background, including the main character(s), for example: *Once upon a time, there was/were… who lived in/near…*
  ● **the start-up**, when events begin to happen, for example: *Early one morning/One fine day/One dark, stormy night…*
  ● **the main story**, when repetitive events build up to a climax (this is the longest section of the story), for example: time connectives like *then, next, meanwhile, eventually* and other useful connectives such as *unfortunately*
  ● **the ending**, when everything is resolved, for example: time connectives like *finally, at last* and problem-solving connectives such as *fortunately, luckily.*

● When devising actions to go with your story, use special actions to highlight these key language features, for instance:
  ● put one arm in the air every time you use a time connective
  ● put both arms in the air whenever you use a problem-solving connective
  ● make a left–right rippling movement with your hand when you use a word that introduces an extra 'chunk' of information into a sentence, such as *who, while, whenever.*
Use the same actions for specific sorts of words and structures every time you tell a story.

You Can... Use listen–imitate–innovate for creative writing

Good writing depends on well-constructed sentences. We can use children's listening skills to provide them with a repertoire of sentence patterns on which they can innovate in their own writing.

Thinking points

- All too often, sentence level work is about grammatical terminology – nouns and verbs, phrases and clauses – and involves tedious written exercises. In most cases, this makes not one jot of difference to children's writing. The technique described opposite uses minimal terminology and involves no time-consuming writing. Instead, it alerts children's ear to patterns of language that they can use to express their own ideas. By teaching children to listen, we can also teach them to write.

Tips, ideas and activities

- When you are reading with children, look out for sentence constructions at an appropriate level to improve the quality of their writing, for example:
  - for Year 3, a sentence opening with a 'where chunk':
    Deep in the undergrowth, a rat was keeping watch.
  - for Year 6, a sentence opening with an '-ing clause', for example:
    Throwing the keys down on the table, he raced upstairs.

- Read the sentence to the children so they can *listen*. Then ask them to *imitate* by saying it with you a few times. You can jazz this up by asking them to say it softly, loudly, in an American, Scottish, cockney accent, etc. Then give an illustration of how you can *innovate* on one bit of the pattern, for example:
  - *High on the hill, a rat was keeping watch.*
  - *Cramming the money into his pocket, he raced upstairs.*

- Give talking partners a minute or so to come up with other innovations, and collect them, for example:
  - *Far in the East... Down in the burrow... Up on the cupboard...*
  - *Gobbling down his lunch... Spraying her hair with glitter...*

  In the same way, try innovating on the whole sentence:
  - *Far in the East, a child was born.*
  - *Spraying her hair with glitter, Mandy set off for the party.*

- This activity should create an auditory echo in children's heads that they can draw on in their writing. To help ram it home, be sure to use the construction yourself in your next session of shared writing.

You Can... **Link listening to cross-curricular literacy**

Just as listening to stories is a bridge to writing fiction, drama and role play can be a bridge to cross-curricular writing

Tips, ideas and activities

● Before asking children to write a particular type of non-fiction text, provide an opportunity to talk – and listen to – the appropriate language. Role-play of various kinds is appropriate for different text types:

- recount – radio or TV news report of a specific event (it could be an event from history)
- report – descriptive television documentary, such as a wildlife programme
- instruction – TV chef, house-designer, DIY expert, and so on
- explanation – teacher or documentary explaining a process or phenomenon
- persuasion – speech on behalf of a pressure group or interest group
- discussion – balanced debate.

● Ensure children have access to the facts/information they need to carry off the role-play. It helps to jot down information in the form of 'memory-joggers' (brief notes, diagrams, pictures, symbols) on the relevant skeleton framework (see page 10 and photocopiable page 58). Children can then use visual and spatial imagery to access information as they speak.

● You can also use other listening activities described in this book to ensure they have access to important vocabulary (see page 12) and useful language constructions (see page 41).

● Some children like to write themselves a complete script for a role-play activity of this kind. There is no reason why they should not – if they work on a computer, they should be able to edit it into a piece of written work later.

You Can... **Teach non-fiction language structures through listening**

Just as children need to listen – imitate – innovate *to develop their control of language for writing stories, they also need auditory echoes of non-fiction language structures.*

Thinking points

● Different types of non-fiction writing rely on different sorts of language constructions. For instance, in general:

● *recount* involves the language of sequence (and, often, consequence)

● *non-chronological report* includes examples and definitions, and often involves the language of comparison

● *instructions* use sequential language and imperatives

● *explanations* involve the same language factors as report, along with the language of sequence, cause and effect

● *persuasion* includes persuasive devices, and often constructions that delineate a number of points

● *discussion* involves the language of balanced argument.

Tips, Ideas and activities

● When you want to familiarise children with a language construction that they are likely to need in writing across the curriculum, introduce it orally in the way described for fiction constructions on page 41. For instance, if you were introducing the language of exemplification, you could:

● let children *listen* to a sample sentence, for example:
*Many types of dog are kept as pets, **such as** poodles, collies and Bedlington terriers.*

● Ask them to *imitate* the construction by repeating it several times.

● Give them the chance to *innovate* on it. This is often easier with non-fiction, because all you have to do is change the subject matter to something with which the children are familiar, for example:
Many types of equipment are kept in a kitchen, such as...
Many animals are reared on farms, such as...

● With older children, you may wish to introduce a range of available constructions, so they can vary their sentence structures, for example:
*Many types of dog are kept as pets, **including** poodles, collies and Bedlington terriers.*
*Many types of dog are kept as pets, **for example**: poodles, collies and Bedlington terriers.*
*Many types of dog are kept as pets, **for instance**: poodles, collies and Bedlington terriers.*

Write the range of 'exemplification words' on the board, and let the children try them out in their own sentences. If lots of different children try it with lots of different content, there will be plenty of opportunities for children to hear and internalise the words and patterns.

● There are collections of words and many suggestions for activities in *Speaking Frames* by Sue Palmer (see page 13).

You Can... **Integrate listening into classroom routines**

Well-established and sensible classroom routines create a sense of security for children and their regular repetition makes them ideal vehicles for listening skills.

Thinking points

- Routine and ritual are important for children because they help create secure neural networks into which other learning can be integrated. So children from homes where there is not a great deal of routine and stability benefit especially from daily rituals. If these are linked to listening skills, it should help them settle into the listening ethos of school education.

- The suggestions opposite are only starting points. Once you are aware of the listening needs of your class, you can think up appropriate activities to develop the underpinning skills. Integrating these into classroom routines provides a perfect opportunity for repetitive practice.

Tips, ideas and activities

- Use the period when children are arriving in the classroom as an opportunity to familiarise them with music you intend to use in the near future (see page 32) by having it playing quietly in the background.

- Start the school day with an activity that helps children tune into listening and prepares them for working together. Music is an ideal vehicle for this, for example:
  - a short aerobics session to develop physical coordination and control (see page 27).
  - a short singing session (see page 30).

- With younger children, use songs and chants to signal changeover times during the day. Instead of calling them to attention, train them to join in when they hear you start a particular song or chant. As they join in, they begin the relevant activity, for example:
  - This chant by teacher Linda Caroe, to rally children for storytime:
    One, two, three, four, come and sit down on the floor
    Five, six, seven, eight, hurry up and don't be late
    One, two, three, four, are your bottoms on the floor?
    Five, six, seven, eight, settle down and sit up straight.
  - Made-up songs, like this one for 'Tidy Up Time':
    It's time to tidy up, it's time to tidy up,
    Ee aye addio, it's time to tidy up.
    We're clearing up the mess... and so on
    We're putting stuff away... and so on
    We're putting up the chairs... and so on

- Have a regular time for sharing the class novel (see page 33) – perhaps at the end of the school day, or immediately after break or lunchtime to give a motivating reason for children to come in and settle down quietly.

- Display a visual timetable in the classroom (see page 46), so that at any time in the day children know what to expect next.

You Can... Use signs and symbols to save airspace

If we want children to listen to us, we have to be careful how we use our voices – putting some information into the visual field frees up the airspace for more important information.

Thinking points

● While repetition is essential for children's learning, it is *their* repetition that counts, not yours. If you repeatedly explain aspects of class organisation or nag children about behaviour, they will switch off because this is not the sort of thing that motivates them. You want them to associate your voice with interesting, relevant listening experiences, not miserable ones.

● Holding up a picture or symbol to show the behaviour you require (like those on photocopiable page 61) can be more effective than a verbal instruction. Visual directions, such as street signs, often elicit a more immediate, automatic response, and can be less wounding to children's self-esteem.

● Contemporary children – brought up in a multimedia society – also tend to find visual cues easy to remember, so they are a helpful aid to classroom management.

TIMETABLE

BREAK

LUNCH

BREAK

Tips, ideas and activities

● Keep your voice for the listening activities that matter. Use visual alternatives to cover more workaday aspects of classroom life, such as organisation and behaviour management. For example:

○ use actions like holding up your hand to tell children silence is required – as they see you, they mimic your movements and fall silent

○ hold up or point to pictures, signs and symbols (see photocopiable page 61) to remind children of behavioural rules, rather than repeatedly explaining or nagging (for example, the listening rules).

● Make a visual timetable like the one shown in the illustration to show the events of the school day. Each day, attach cards with pictures/symbols (see examples on photocopiable page 61) in L>R sequence to indicate the events that children can expect during that section of the day. Encourage the children to keep an eye on the timetable so they are mentally prepared for each event. Boys particularly find it reassuring to know what is coming next.

● Display clear, highly visual posters for key instructions, such as 'Have a go at spelling' and 'How to find a spelling word' (see photocopiable page 60). Rather than constantly repeating these instructions (which eventually just sounds like nagging), just point to the poster and say: *And don't forget…*

● Use symbols for behaviour management – pictures or coloured cards that you and any other adults in the classroom can carry with you. Like a football referee, you and any other adults in the classroom can show these to rule-breakers rather than speaking (when someone is not attending, catch his eye by waving the 'Look at the teacher' card).

You Can... **Use listening games as 'fillers'**

There are many games that develop specific attentional or listening skills which are ideal to fill in the odd few minutes in the hall, playground or classroom.

Thinking points

- It is no surprise that so many children's games emphasise listening skills. Play is the natural way for children to learn, and effective listening has always been an essential lesson. Nowadays, however, we are inclined to emphasise the visual over the auditory, and this sort of game is neglected.

- There are many commercially-produced listening games on CD, such as 'Sound Bingo', which can be great fun and very helpful. But be sure you know which aspects of listening they are meant to refine.

Tips, ideas and activities

- For developing physical control and balance, as well as discriminative listening, use simple Stop Go games, like 'Dodgems' (see page 7) and 'Musical Statues' or 'Traffic Lights', where children move around pretending to be cars until you shout *Red* (they stop), *Green* (they can go) or *Amber* (they slow down).

- Most Year 3 and 4 children also enjoy 'Sleeping Lions', which also introduces them to the joy of silence:
  - Three or four children are hunters and the rest are lions, lying still on the ground to sleep (with eyes shut).
  - At a signal from the teacher, the hunters tiptoe among the lions. Each chooses a lion to touch (stroking, tapping, and so on) until the signal to withdraw.
  - The lions who have been touched have to guess which hunter touched them. If right, they swap places and become a hunter.

- To help them learn the importance of listening carefully, play 'Simon Says', where the teacher gives instructions, but children must only follow them if they are preceded by the words *Simon says*.

- To develop mental imaging skills (see page 10), play occasional miming games, for instance 'Adverbs', where one child goes out, the rest choose an adverb (for example, *slinkily, cheerfully, exhaustedly*) and when the child returns, he or she gives tasks to members of the class which they have to do 'in the manner of the adverb'.

- Play cumulative listening games, such as:
  - *Mrs Brown went to town and she bought a…*
  - *I went on holiday and I packed a…*
  where each child recites the list as it stands and adds another item. These are ideal fillers for the odd five minutes. You can:
  - make the lists alphabetical (*apple, book, candle*), aiding memorisation through organisation
  - turn it into a team game, and continue until one child cannot remember the list – but be careful to keep up the poor soul's spirits!

You Can... Develop listening skills in maths lessons

Children's success in mental maths depends on their ability to combine active listening, mental imaging and auditory memory.

Thinking points

- Neuroscientists suggest that the major skills involved In mathematical ability are:
  - an appreciation of quantity (which includes spatial ability – and the capacity to imagine quantities and spatial relationships)
  - an understanding of the visual and verbal representations of numbers.

Mental imaging – linked to hearing and registering words – underpins both of these skills.

- For many decades now, we have discouraged children from counting on their fingers – why? Fingers are ready to hand and easy to count. The reason for the decimal system is that we have this number of bodily attributes. There is a direct neurological link between the fingertips and the prefrontal cortex of the brain – the part associated with focused concentration, planning and multi-tasking. It seems likely that making use of this link should help with learning number.

Tips, ideas and activities

- There are many listening sub-skills involved in mental maths, and children need to be competent in all of them in order to do mental calculations. If they are not, the activity will be very stressful indeed, and could mean they build up a resistance to maths.

- Mental imaging is particularly significant (see Thinking Points), so give lots of practice in:
  - mental imaging of quantities (for example, *Close your eyes and imagine six stars, then give a clap for each star… Take two stars away and clap for each star left.*)
  - mental imaging of spatial organisation (for example, help children imagine numbers as shapes, as on a dice)
  - using simple diagrams/visual mnemonics which can be manipulated mentally throughout your maths teaching, and help children internalise these.

- Do not worry about children using their fingers for counting if this helps – it may be that it aids mental imagery.

- Since mental maths involves such a rallying of listening and mathematical skills, take care to build children's capacity over time. Listening stamina for so much mental effort can take a long time to develop. So start with just one question at a time, then build to two, and so on. Put children who are having difficulties into a smaller group and give them extra time and help.

- There are many excellent mental maths activities in *Maths Call (Year R to 6)* by Peter Clark (Harper Collins Publishers).

You Can... Develop listening skills in history, geography, science...

Listening is a significant element of teaching across the curriculum. Once you are aware of what is involved, you can target specific listening skills in every lesson.

Thinking points

● In the past, teachers did not have to worry about incorporating the teaching of listening skills into their work across the curriculum – we assumed that listening ability developed naturally. Often, it did, but sometimes it did not – as was often the case for disadvantaged children from noisy, language-poor homes.

● For this reason, visual teaching techniques such as skeleton frameworks have often proved popular with low-achieving children – they are less reliant on listening skills and do not feel so much like 'hard work'. And sometimes (especially in science), well-composed skeleton notes are a better record of what has been learned than a written version. However, if we are to help all children learn to listen, we also have to use visual techniques as a bridge to improved listening skills.

Tips, ideas and activities

● Help children build a repertoire of mental images of the structures that underpin our thought processes. The skeletons for writing (see photocopiable page 58) can act as:
  ● visual icons for particular structures of thought
  ● note-taking devices during study across the curriculum
  ● 'carrier bags' to transport cross-curricular information to the literacy lesson, where it can become the basis of children's non-fiction writing.

Whatever you are teaching, use the appropriate skeleton framework in your explanations, and encourage children to do so too (making skeleton notes on something you have just learned is an excellent task for talking partners).

● Encourage children to put 'memory joggers' on their skeleton frameworks (odd words, pictures, abbreviations, symbols – anything that will jog their memory about what they have learned).

● Then ensure children acquire the necessary technical vocabulary through focused teaching, including:
  ● opportunities for frequent repetition of the word
  ● immediate opportunities to use the words in context (see also page 12 and skeleton note-making, above).

● Provide models of appropriate language constructions, and activities to put 'auditory echoes' of these constructions in children's heads (see page 13). Then, when it is time for children to write about what they have learned, tell them to *Turn your memory joggers into sentences.*

● For more information about how to use skeleton teaching frameworks, see *How to Teach Non-Fiction Writing at Key Stage Two* by Sue Palmer (David Fulton Books) and *The Complete Skeleton Book* by Sue Palmer (TTS Group Ltd).

● You might find that, occasionally, the quickest way to record some necessary information in pupils' books is a short dictation (see page 38).

You Can... **Teach listening through PE and drama**

PE and formal drama lessons involve children attending to the teacher's oral directions at the same time as thinking about what they are going to do and coordinating their movements.

Thinking points

● Listening skills are, of course, only one element in learning – the brain is a hugely complex organ, and every 'learning incident' involves simultaneous activity in a multitude of neural networks. In PE and drama, children frequently have to link auditory stimuli to physical response, so make sure you:

- recognise the listening skills involved, and focus on developing these as well as other elements in the lesson
- use other techniques where possible (such as visual models) to lessen the auditory load for learning.

● Many teachers are edgy about drama, thinking lessons could drift out of control. In fact, once you have established basic class control, drama is such a motivating activity that children often behave better while in character than they do in more sedentary activities.

Tips, Ideas and Activities

● When planning PE or drama lessons, bear in mind the listening implications. For instance:

- all activities that develop physical control and balance (especially cross-lateral movements) can help children with poor coordination become better at sitting still in class
- stop/go activities mean children have to discriminate a foreground sound such as a whistle (or a range of sounds or verbal instructions) against background noise
- opportunities for children to listen to and internalise a sequence of instructions can help develop auditory memory and listening stamina
- responding physically (and in space) to auditory stimuli – such as music, your role-play instructions or narration – provides opportunities for children to develop their powers of mental imagery.

● Watch out for children who perform poorly in these areas. May their problems be due to poor listening skills, rather than inadequacies in PE or drama? If so, are there ways you can help improve these skills? For example:

- in PE, setting up an 'assault course' that involves plenty of crawling and climbing (cross-lateral movements)
- in drama, providing opportunities for mime to develop visual imagery
- in PE and drama, gradually building up the number of instructions you give at any time, starting with a sequence of two, then building to three.

● To avoid over-playing the auditory channel when introducing a specific drama technique (for example, role-play in groups, hot-seating, freeze-frame or Conscience Alley) use video to demonstrate what it looks like. A useful resource is the training video in the NLS/QCA 'Speaking and Listening' box, issued to all schools in England in 2004, which contains clips of all the techniques listed above – or you could video your own classes for use later as 'demonstration lessons'. Show a short clip of children engaging in a specific drama technique, and then discuss how the class could use it to develop their understanding of the topic you are currently exploring. You could record illustrations of PE activities for future use in the same way.

You Can... **Teach listening through role-play**

Teaching children to listen also involves providing opportunities for them to listen to each other. Role-play areas are an excellent setting for this, as they draw on children's natural instinct to play.

Thinking points

● The use of role play areas for older children used to be common 30 years ago, but has fallen out of fashion – perhaps because it looks too much like fun. Play of this kind is, however, a powerful learning tool and the element of fun means children usually become highly engaged in the learning.

● Nowadays also, there is a perception that older primary children may think such an area 'babyish'. Contemporary children often have a veneer of sophistication, gained from watching a great many 'sassy' teenagers on TV programmes. However, they are still children, with a deep inbuilt need to play. If you use the art/DT approach suggested above, role-play usually arises naturally out of their ownership of the environment.

Tips, ideas and activities

● When planning for any subject or topic work, try always to provide a relevant role-play area. For example, if you are studying the Second World War, you might set up an air-raid shelter (a corrugated card roof suspended from wall/furniture in a corner of the classroom?).

● Creating this area provides many opportunities for research work, art, DT and ICT, and thus for talk around the topic. For instance, for the air-raid shelter, children could research the items that would be kept there, find or make artefacts and costumes, produce documents such as ration books on computer, and so on. Other historical periods offer similar possibilities, such as an Egyptian tomb, a Roman forum (throw in a few sheets for togas), or a room in a Tudor or Victorian home. As well as providing a focus for children's informal play, groups could develop more formal presentations to act out in the 'set' for the rest of the class.

● Other role-play areas popular with older children are science labs, space or weather stations, travel agents, newspaper offices and TV studios. These offer ways of integrating drama activities into science, geography, PHSE and citizenship.

● If you really cannot find space, or to ring the changes, 'small world' or doll's house versions can be created in cat litter trays or built from cardboard boxes. Children can people these with plastic figures or home-made pipe-cleaner puppets – and once they have become involved, even hardened Year 6 children can often be found providing the voices for their 'small worlders'.

You Can... **Develop listening skills in collaborative group work**

Another important opportunity for children to listen to each other is during group activities, whether it is structured or arises naturally from self-chosen play.

Thinking points

● Children also benefit hugely from:
  ○ unstructured loosely supervised free time when they can develop social listening skills naturally through self-chosen interactions
  ○ self-chosen activities (such as creating materials for or 'acting' a role-play area – see page 51) which provide opportunities for natural social interaction.

Apart from intervention for reasons of safety or noise-abatement, they will gain far more from these activities if adults leave them to it.

● Children who cannot listen during large group or class activities are unlikely to benefit greatly from *unsupervised* structured group work, and their behaviour may prevent other children from benefiting too. They first need to learn the skills of listening through the sorts of activities described throughout this book, including supervised group and class work such as circle time.

Tips, ideas and activities

● Once children have acquired basic listening skills (including active social listening), introduce independent structured group work, in which they can practise their speaking and listening skills with each other. This includes:
  ○ focused group discussion about subjects you are studying, which provides opportunities for children to use new words and knowledge in context. Such discussions are always more effective if you provide open-ended questions, for example:
  What would life be like if there was no electricity?
  Decide which of these eminent Victorians is the odd one out.
  Rank these statements about sustainability in order of importance.
  ○ drama or role-play where children work as a group to devise and polish a short performance for the rest of the class
  ○ Readers' Theatre activities, where a group of children take a short, familiar text and devise a presentation of it, using a variety of voices, voice combinations and sound effects.

● Group work needs plenty of discussion beforehand, to decide on classroom rules and procedures – use the techniques described for the Listening Classroom (page 14) to establish these.

● For children who are unable to work collaboratively in this way, use assessment procedures (see page 55 and photocopiable page 62) to decide which aspects of listening to target specifically – in an incremental way – to build up their skills. Give them plenty of opportunities to work in supervised groups (the more difficulties they have, the smaller the group) where they can try the same sort of activities as other children, but with adult support.

You Can... Integrate visual ICT into your teaching of listening

Too great a reliance on screen-based learning may inhibit listening skills rather than promote them. Ensure that any use of ICT is productive and encourages focused listening.

Thinking points

● On the whole, the message from neuroscience and developmental psychology is that children benefit more from real-life first-hand activity than from sedentary, screen-based experience. For satisfactory cognitive development, many first-hand experiences need to be mediated by talk, either with adults or peers – and this, of course, involves listening.

Tips, ideas and activities

● Always think carefully about how you use electronic whiteboards and other screen-based teaching devices. Used wisely, they are a magnificent resource, but too much time spent staring at screens can deaden children's other attentional skills.

● Since children learn by imitation, video is an excellent resource for demonstrating the sort of behaviour you want to encourage, for example, drama or PE activities (see page 50), paired talk or group work – there are plenty of National Literacy or Numeracy Strategy video clips illustrating a range of classroom techniques. I have also come across teachers using these videos to demonstrate general classroom behaviour (not a bad idea, since children believe what they see on TV and their experience of TV classrooms is usually limited to *Grange Hill*).

● Video can also be helpful in developing role-play – a TV drama set in a particular period, a documentary about a particular culture, or TV footage of events in the news can be used to provide background information, and – with repeated viewing to check on facts – relevant vocabulary and turns of phrase.

● Visual ICT makes a great focus for group work, with children making Powerpoint presentations about what they have learned, pages for a website, or TV 'newscasts' or 'documentaries'.

● All of these illustrate how helpful ICT can be in developing focused listening. But when using an ICT resource, do keep in mind your specific teaching objective and the underlying listening skills involved. Beware of resources that promise listening skills, but merely keep children entertained and/or occupied with fairly pointless tasks.

You Can... Use auditory ICT to develop listening skills

The current emphasis on screen-based learning means many teachers have forgotten that there is a wealth of auditory ICT resources, which can be used to teach listening skills across the curriculum.

Thinking points

● Few children these days listen to radio. In the middle of the twentieth century, many children from disadvantaged backgrounds were probably alerted to literate language patterns by the constant presence of radio in their homes. But audio resources (story tapes while children are engaged in quiet, practical work; poems to listen to and enjoy again and again; audio contributions to cross-curricular study) could be used in contemporary classrooms in the same way.

● However, beware of falling into the trap described by one teacher I met. 'Children today,' she proclaimed, 'are a rewind generation! They know they can always press the rewind button so they don't bother listening the first time!' Perhaps you should preface most audio listening with the instruction: 'Listen very carefully. I shall play zis only vonce!'

Tips, ideas and activities

● Audiotapes and CDs are ready-made listening materials, providing commercially-produced music, poetry and stories, which can be used to support activities listed throughout this book.

● There are also audio materials that support work across the curriculum:
  ● BBC School Radio programmes (www.bbc.co.uk/schoolradio) which have cross-curricular resources for all age groups, many of which are now available on the internet
  ● BT Education's teaching materials (www.bt.com)
  ● 'oral history' websites, such as audio files on the Imperial War Museum's website or the oral history section of the BBC's Weather department.

All of these provide:
  ● opportunities to bring other voices into the classroom besides your own
  ● a highly-focused reason for listening
  ● chances for *you* to model active listening to the class.

● Look out for further devices that could be helpful in developing the skills we have discussed, such as:
  ● mini-recording devices that allow children to record sounds or their own voices
  ● amplifiers for use in group or classwork, such as karaoke machines or mini-microphones (some teachers use these as the 'special object' passed around to signify whose turn it is during circle time – and the child can talk into the microphone)
  ● resources on the internet, such as the CBBC website, where there are often music or listening games (but see these as a fun extension of your real-life listening activities, not as any sort of substitute).

You Can... Assess children's progress

Until the government devises tests and targets for listening skills, teachers are free to assess their children's development in sensible, useful, non-time-consuming ways.

Thinking points

Analysing the assessment sheet:

(a)s and (b)s across the board may simply mean the child has not developed listening skills naturally (in which case, you can hope for steady progress using the activities described here). But if there are a great many (a)s, or if the child does not make progress, refer to a speech and language therapist for assessment.

In the following more specific scenarios, difficulties could again simply be due to poor listening skills, so try the appropriate activities. But if the child does not make progress and is still scoring:

● (a)s and (b)s specifically on 1 and 2, it could indicate dyspraxia – check with Senco to be on the safe side.

● (a)s and (b)s on question 2 onwards, he or she could have hearing problems (either general or intermittent hearing loss) – check with parents and/or refer to the school doctor or audiometrician.

● (a)s on questions 3, 4, 5 and 6, he or she could be on the autistic spectrum – check with the Senco.

● (a)s on questions 4, 5 and 6, he or she could have emotional difficulties – perhaps arrange a meeting with parents and the Senco.

● (a)s and (b)s specifically on questions 7 and 8, this could be an indicator of dyslexia – check with the Senco.

Tips, ideas and activities

● If children's listening seems to be developing satisfactorily, do not bother with formal assessment. You will be able to spot whether they have:

- physical control and balance (through their ability to stand/sit still when required
- discriminative listening skills (through their performance in games)
- social listening skills (in their general social interaction and behaviour in circle time)
- good auditory memory (by their ability to memorise songs, rhymes and stories)
- listening stamina (by their tolerance of listening activities).

If a child is giving no cause for concern, just keep on with focused, incremental teaching until you no longer need to teach listening skills, but can use established skills to underpin learning across the curriculum.

● During everyday activities, concentrate your attention on those children who are having difficulties. Use the rule-of-thumb checklist on photocopiable page 62 to get an indication of where problems might lie (see box left), and provide more incremental practice of the skills that seem to be giving them trouble. But if you are in any doubt, always refer children on to the relevant expert. As the box shows, in a small proportion of cases, an inability to listen may be the result of a physical or developmental disorder.

● As for children's phonemic awareness, keep an eye on the list on page 51 and, if a child seems to be having trouble with a particular sound, give plenty of practice of an appropriate rhyme. But if you have any real cause for concern, contact a speech and language therapist for an assessment.

Recommended poems and rhymes

Punctuation Street Rap

You gotta punk and chunk to make that
text make sense:
Put a little full stop after ev'ry sun tence,
An ex-clam-ation mark for ex-clam-ation,
A question mark for in-terr-ogation,
Three dots show that it's incomplete —
That's how to chunk text on Punctuation
Street.

You gotta punk and chunk to make
your sentences clear;
Commas show the way around
your ideas.
Need to keep words apart? —
a dash can hack it;
To cordon them off, you need brackets.
To hold words together a hyphen is
sweet —
That's how to chunk sentences
on Punctuation Street.

Two vivid poems for mental imaging:

Windy Nights

Whenever the moon and stars are set,
Whenever the wind is high,
All night long in the dark and wet,
A man goes riding by.
Late in the night when the fires are out
Why does he gallop and gallop about?

Whenever the trees are crying aloud,
And ships are tossed at sea,
By on the highway, low and loud,
By at the gallop goes he.
By at the gallop he goes, and then
By he comes back at the gallop again!

Robert Louis Stevenson

The Flying Dutchman

We met the Flying Dutchman
By midnight he came,
His hull was all of hellfire,
His sails were all aflame;
Fire on the maintop,
Fire on the bow,
Fire on the gun deck,
Fire down below.

Four and twenty dead men,
Those were the crew,
The Devil on the bowsprit,
Fiddled as she flew.
We gave her the broadside,
Right in the dip,
Just like a candle,
Went out the ship.

Charles Godfrey Leland

Recommended songs

The Spelling Song (to the tune of *Knees Up Mother Brown*)
Chorus: Look say cover write check (yeah!)
Look say cover write check (yeah!)
Look say cover
Look say cover
Look say cover write check (yeah!)

Look for family links
Look for letter strings
Double letters
Trouble letters
Look, look, look and THINK!

Chorus

SAAAAAY... syllables loud and clear
Say vowels so you can hear
Don't forget a
Single letter
Say and use your EARS!

Chorus

Cover and write it plain
Check that word again
You can tell a
Brilliant speller
By eye, ear, hand and brain!

Chorus

The Sentence Song (to the tune of *My Bonnie Lies Over the Ocean*)
Oh, sentences break up your writing,
They show where to stop for a rest,
They help make your writing exciting,
They help make your stories the best.

Chorus:

Sentence... sentence...
Oh, sentences make text make sense, make sense.
Sentence... sentence...
Oh, sentences make text make sense.

So tell me, how long is a sentence?
And is it the same as a line?
No – it can be longer or shorter –
As long as it makes sense, it's fine.

Chorus

It starts with a capital letter.
It finishes with a full stop.
It makes writing clearer and better –
So come on, then, right from the top:

Chorus

Skeletons for the six non-fiction text types

Recount – chronological retelling of events

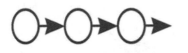

Instructions – sequenced instructions ('how to do something')

Non-chronological report – description of the characteristics of something ('how things are')

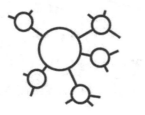

Explanation – sequential technical explanation ('how/why things work or happen')

Persuasion – opinion or argument ('why you should think this')

Discussion – reasoned argument ('the case for and against...')

Letter to parents

Dear Parent or Carer,

Songs and Rhymes

Every week throughout this year, your child will bring home a short song or rhyme to learn by heart. We would be very grateful if you could help with this, by singing or chanting along with your child till s/he knows it.

Just before bedtime and first thing in the morning are good times to practise. And as your child builds up a repertoire, could you have a 'Song and Rhyme Time' session every so often and revise the lot (perhaps in the car, or to fill in time at a bus stop)?

The rhymes and songs don't take long to learn because they're quite short, but it could help your child's education a great deal. They are an enjoyable way of developing an essential learning skill known as auditory memory. In the past, most children developed their auditory memory fairly naturally, but in today's multimedia world, this often doesn't happen.

The better their auditory memory, the easier children find it to spell words correctly, remember facts, solve maths problems and do many other basic educational tasks.
Thank you very much for your help.

Yours sincerely,

Class Teacher

Visual reminders for classroom procedures

Have a go!

When you are writing, have a go at spelling.

When you have finished, read your work. If you think a spelling is wrong, try to put it right.

Check your spelling

Underline misspelled words in <u>pensel</u>.
↓
Have another go on scrap paper.
↙   ↘
That looks right!   Hmm, still unsure?
↓   ↓
Correct it in your text.   Try
                        ↓

↓   ↓   ↓   ↓
the class list   a handheld   asking a   a dictionary
of high   spellchecker or good speller   or spelling
frequency   spellcheck on the   dictionary
words   computer

Cue cards

Activity cards:

Behaviour management cards:

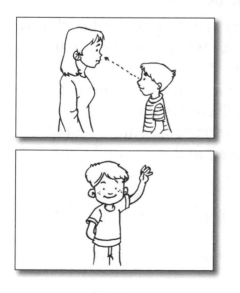

Listening assessment sheet

1. I am generally in control of my movements:
   a) hardly any of the time
   b) part of the time
   c) most of the time
   d) all of the time

2. I can:
   a) not sit still at all
   b) sit still for a short period when engaged in a task that interests me
   c) sit still for extended periods when the task interests me
   d) sit still when the teacher asks me to

3. I make eye contact:
   a) when someone physically directs my face to the speaker
   b) when I hear someone call my name
   c) when someone is speaking directly to me
   d) with the teacher when she is talking to the class

4. I can take my turn in conversations:
   a) never
   b) in directed one-to-one activities with an adult
   c) in structured situations such as circle time
   d) in general, during social interactions with others

5. When we play listening games, I:
   a) don't follow the rules
   b) can follow the rules as long as they suit me
   c) take a long time to learn the rules
   d) learn and follow rules quite quickly

6. In circle time:
   a) I stay silent and/or look bewildered
   b) I copy what others say, but rather hesitantly
   c) I join in, sometimes copying, but sometimes making my own contributions
   d) I join in confidently, and make innovative contributions

7. I find learning rhymes and songs:
   a) very difficult and take a very long time to remember them, if ever
   b) quite difficult and I muddle words, lose the rhythm, don't remember rhymes
   c) reasonably easy as long as I get lots of repetition
   d) pretty easy

8. When the class is joining in with stories:
   a) I look uninterested or bewildered
   b) I make movements with my mouth, but don't keep up
   c) I join in and learn the words with plenty of repetition
   d) I learn refrains and repeated words easily, and am soon word-perfect

Index

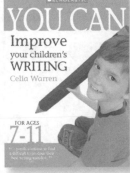

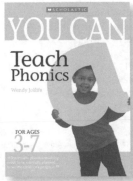